KU-207-951

The Easy Garden

The Easy Garden

Alec Bristow

Mitchell Beazley Limited
London

First published in the UK by Mitchell
Beazley Limited, Artists House,
14/15 Manette Street,
London W1V 5LB.
Designed and produced for Mitchell
Beazley by Reference International.

ISBN 0 85533 124 0

Printed in Great Britain

Contents

Introduction

THIS BOOK is for people who love gardens but do not love gardening. Its aim is to show you how to get the most out of your garden for as little work as possible. The test of an easy garden is that you should get more out of it than you put into it—whether in pleasure, beauty, relaxation, or your own fruit and vegetables. From that point of view far too many gardens are dismal failures, demanding from their owners hours of hard labour but giving far too little in return.

The trouble is that during most of the two or three centuries that the modern garden has taken to develop labour was cheap and plentiful. The ordinary person had no garden at all, except perhaps a patch of ground to grow a few vegetables and herbs. Those who could afford a garden could afford gardeners, and even quite a small establishment would have a head gardener (who never got his hands dirty) and one or two under-gardeners who did the actual work. So the garden was a place where work was created, to keep those hands busy. Miles of hedges were planted in order to be trimmed, ground cleared in order to be dug, and gravel paths laid in order to be constantly weeded. At the same time in the house itself there would be several domestic servants.

Even during the rise of the suburbs over the last seventy-five years, the smallest semi-detached villa used to house at least one servant, and the garden would be looked after by a jobbing gardener, who did all the hard work. Now that servants have disappeared, houses have been redesigned to reduce drudgery. Vacuum cleaners and washing machines have replaced muscle-power, and the result is brighter and better living; the vanishing of cheap labour has forced the average home into the second half of the twentieth century.

Outdoors, however, it is quite another story. As soon as they go into the garden, many people step back a century in time, to a world of hard, monotonous work. Cheap labour in the garden has disappeared even more completely than it has in the house, so present-day garden owners have to rely on their own exertions. All too often they never have time to enjoy their gardens because they are too busy working in them. The purpose of this book is to point out how you can reduce that labour, so that your garden becomes as easy to run as your home.

By good planning, by choosing easy plants, by giving them the best conditions for healthy growth and by preventing troubles before they occur, you can have the sort of garden you really want—your servant and not your master.

The first rule for easy gardens is this: *a little mental effort at the beginning will save a lot of physical effort later on.* That is why the next pages deal with the basic principles of garden design to make life as easy as possible. A pencil is much less tiring to use than a spade, and mistakes made on paper can soon be rubbed out. The tasks that take the most time and effort in the average garden are: weeding, digging, mowing, clipping, staking, watering and pruning. In the chapters that follow, ways are described of cutting each of these operations to a minimum. No garden can ever be entirely effort-free: left to itself it would always eventually go back to the wild, simply because the weeds are better suited to their native soil and climate than their competitors; therefore they are at an enormous advantage over our garden plants, many of which are foreigners, evolved for quite different conditions. However, a great deal can be done to reduce the advantage (a) by choosing plants which are better adapted to our gardens, and (b) by modifying soil and conditions to make them not quite so comfortable for the weeds.

There are many thousands of garden plants on the market. Some varieties are the very best of their kind and give the greatest pleasure and satisfaction for the least trouble. Some, unfortunately, are second-class affairs bearing no comparison with the star performers and still in existence only because they represent an investment of many years ago by plant dealers who are too poor, or mean, or old-fashioned, to get rid of them. Even worse, some inferior varieties exist for no better reason than that they are easy to propagate, and so bring the nurseryman quicker profit from unwary buyers. The tables of recommended varieties in this book list only the very best.

One way to cut down labour is by doing things at the right time, so that one is using nature rather than fighting it. Sometimes this means doing things early; for instance, ground dug in the autumn will be much improved, without human effort, by winter frosts and snow. Sometimes it means doing things later; for instance, a hedge clipped too early may soon need clipping again, but left for another month it may not need clipping again that season. Before we come to garden planning, here is one practical suggestion. When considering what features to have in your garden, always include a seat. If you are too busy working in the garden to be able to spend a good deal of time sitting on that seat, then your garden is not easy enough.

Design for Ease

When it comes to planning your garden, the most important labour-saving tools you can have are paper, pencil and a good piece of india-rubber. Mistakes made on paper can easily be rubbed out and corrected, but mistakes made in the garden itself will take a lot of hard work to put right and may remain with you for ever, causing a great deal of continuous and unnecessary labour. So never skimp the number of hours you spend on planning to begin with; it will save you many times that number of hours later on. A good general rule in starting to make a garden is this: never do any work in the garden itself till you have worked it out in your head first.

To show some examples of how to design an easy garden a few actual plans are given in the next few pages. Do not attempt to copy these. They are only intended to point out some of the principles involved. It is impossible to give you an exact pattern to follow, because no two garden sites are ever the same.

That is true even of a modern housing estate such as the one shown in the map opposite, where part of a large field has been cut up into separate building plots. Many of the houses themselves may be absolutely identical, but their gardens are not. Most of the shapes are different, but even where they are similar their aspects vary and so do the amounts of sun, shelter and shade they receive. If you could have any one of them, which would it be? The answer is not always as simple as it seems. For example, if asked to choose between the sunny side of the street and the shady side, most people would probably pick the sunny side. But in nearly every case they would be wrong. The reason is that on the sunny side the front of the house gets the sun but the back gets no sun, so a terrace or patio there is in constant shadow and therefore not much good for sitting out or sunbathing. Worse, the shadow of the house falls across the back garden—which is usually much bigger and more important than the front garden—and makes it a gloomy place.

So in choosing between plots such as 3 or 4 on the plan and ones such as 8 or 9 opposite, remember: *on the sunny side of the street the back garden gets the shade, but on the shady side of the street the back garden gets the sun.*

Other things that need to be considered are the position of existing trees and the direction of the prevailing wind. Trees in the right place can give much-needed shelter. Those marked A and B on the plan will break the force of north winds in garden 5 and west winds in garden 4. Trees C and D will protect gardens 2 and 3 from north and gardens 1 and 2 from west winds. Tree E will shelter garden 7 from south-east, garden 8 from south, and garden 15 from south-west winds.

On the other hand, trees can rob gardens of light. Trees A and B will shade parts of plots 4 and 5, and trees C and D parts of plots 1 and 2, from the afternoon sun.

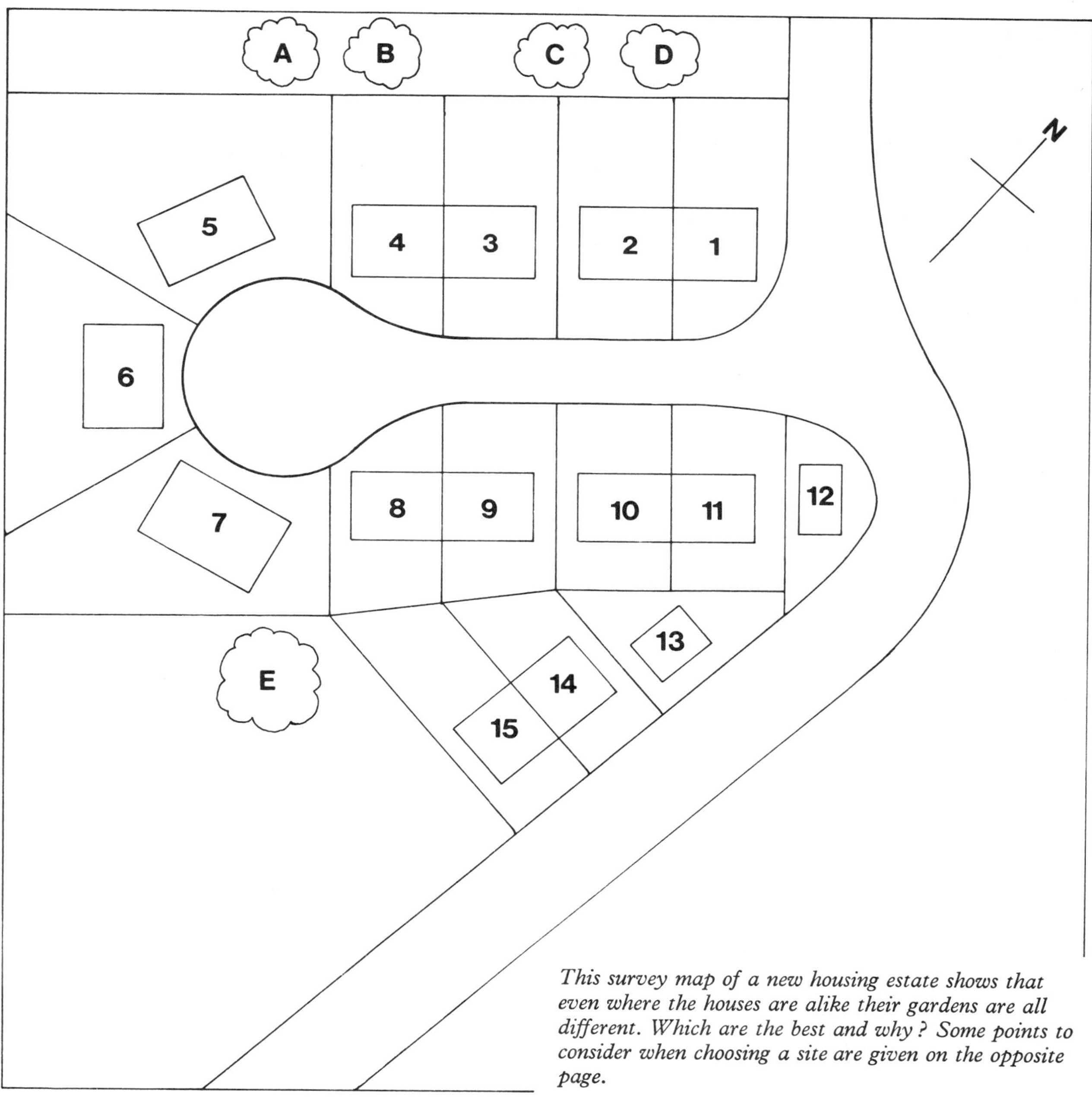

This survey map of a new housing estate shows that even where the houses are alike their gardens are all different. Which are the best and why? Some points to consider when choosing a site are given on the opposite page.

Before you can even begin to think properly about how you are going to arrange your garden, you will need to measure the site and to draw an accurate plan of it on paper.

If it is a new property you may be able to get a copy of the site drawing required by the local planning authority before permission was given for the house to be built. Unfortunately that drawing will not only be on too small a scale but will very likely be quite inaccurate. Planning officers are strict to see that the house is built exactly according to plan, but they rarely check that the boundaries are as shown in the drawing.

So you must draw your own plan of the site as it really is. Make your drawing as large in scale as you can, so that there is plenty of room to mark in all the things you want in your garden. Much the easiest way is to use a sheet of graph-paper; it will save a great deal of time and effort.

Start by measuring the distance from the corner of the house to a point on the far boundary exactly in line with the side of the house (measurement A on the plan opposite). Measure from there to the corner of the boundary (B), from there back to the corner of the house (C), then in turn D, E, F, G and H, as shown. This may seem a lot of bother, but it is necessary because plots of ground are very often crooked rather than straight.

When you have drawn the boundaries on your graph paper according to these measurements, mark in the position of fixed things such as man-hole-covers and trees.

If the ground slopes, measure at different points. The easiest way to do this is with a spirit level, a plank and some pegs, as shown on pages 24 and 25. Mark the levels on the plan, o against the first point, – against lower and + against higher points.

Next make a list of all the things you want in your garden. Then cross out the least important. That will be your first job of weeding out.

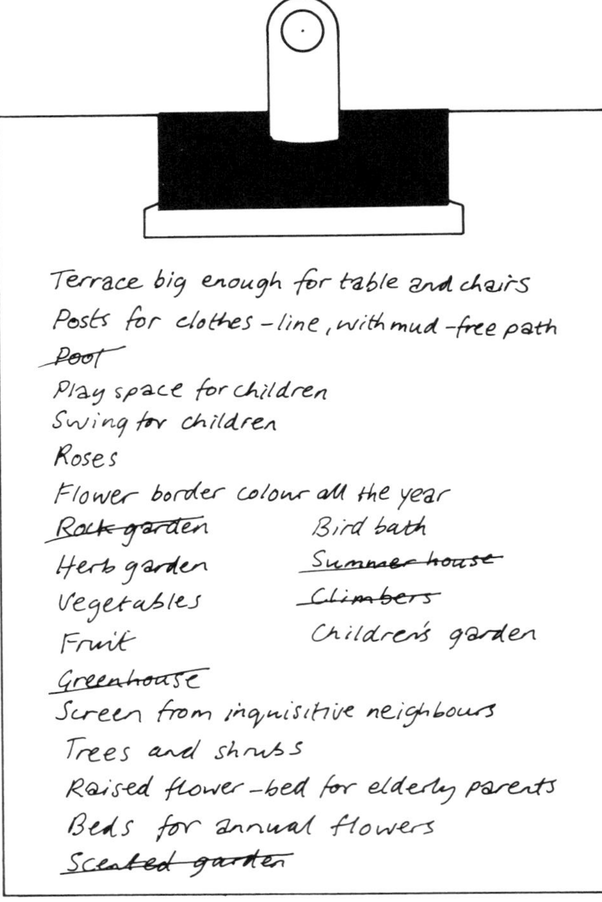

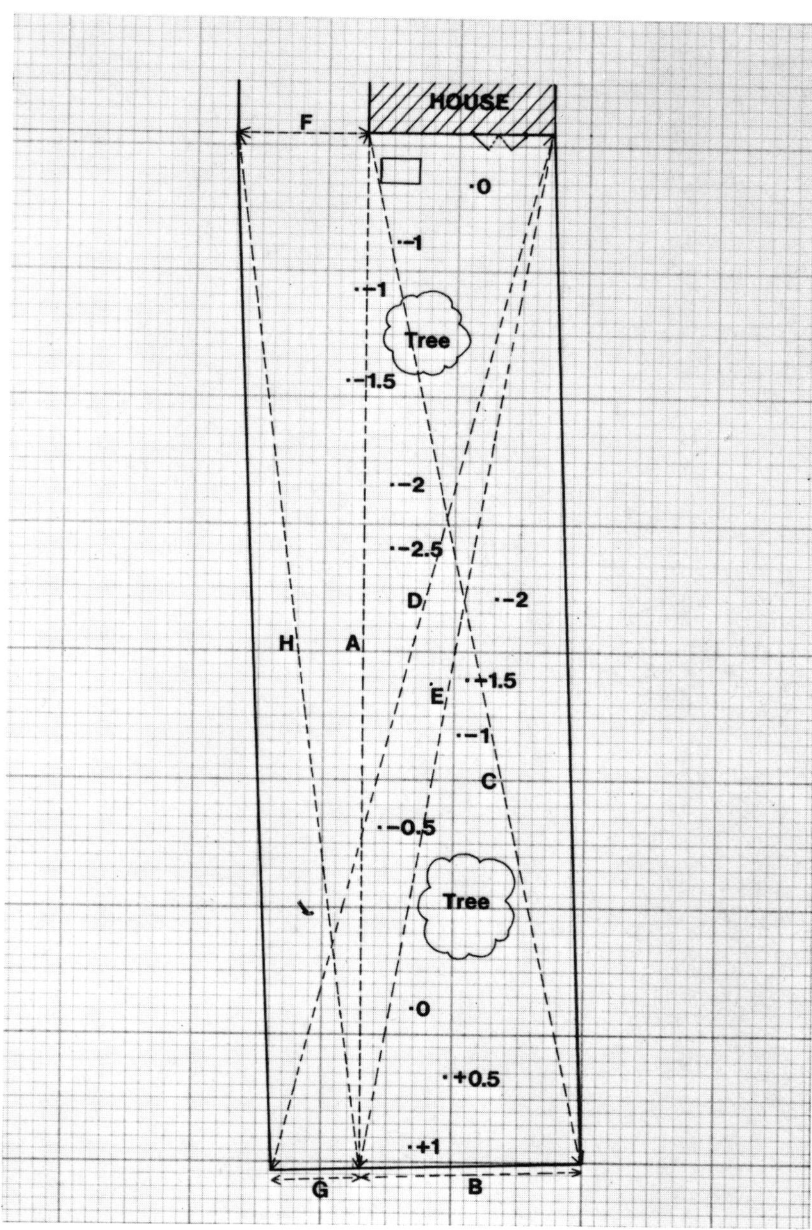

Since plots of ground are rarely rectangular, it is very important to take a number of measurements so that a really accurate plan can be drawn. A description is given on the opposite page of how this should be done. The easiest method of drawing the plan is to transfer the measurements to a large sheet of graph paper and mark in ink the outlines of the house, the position of the boundaries of the plot and existing features, such as trees. Then you can plan out your garden in pencil, altering and rubbing out till you get it just as you want.

An easy garden should not only be easy to manage but easy on the eye. Long, narrow, rectangular plots like that outlined on graph-paper on page 7 look hard and unattractive unless something is done to break the monotony. The best plan in such cases is to divide the plot into separate gardens of different kinds. Here, however, the straight path and beds have done little to soften the hard effect; a long rectangular box has been turned into a series of smaller rectangular boxes. Everything seems to be standing stiffly to attention. The result looks like a garden to be worked at rather than one to be enjoyed.

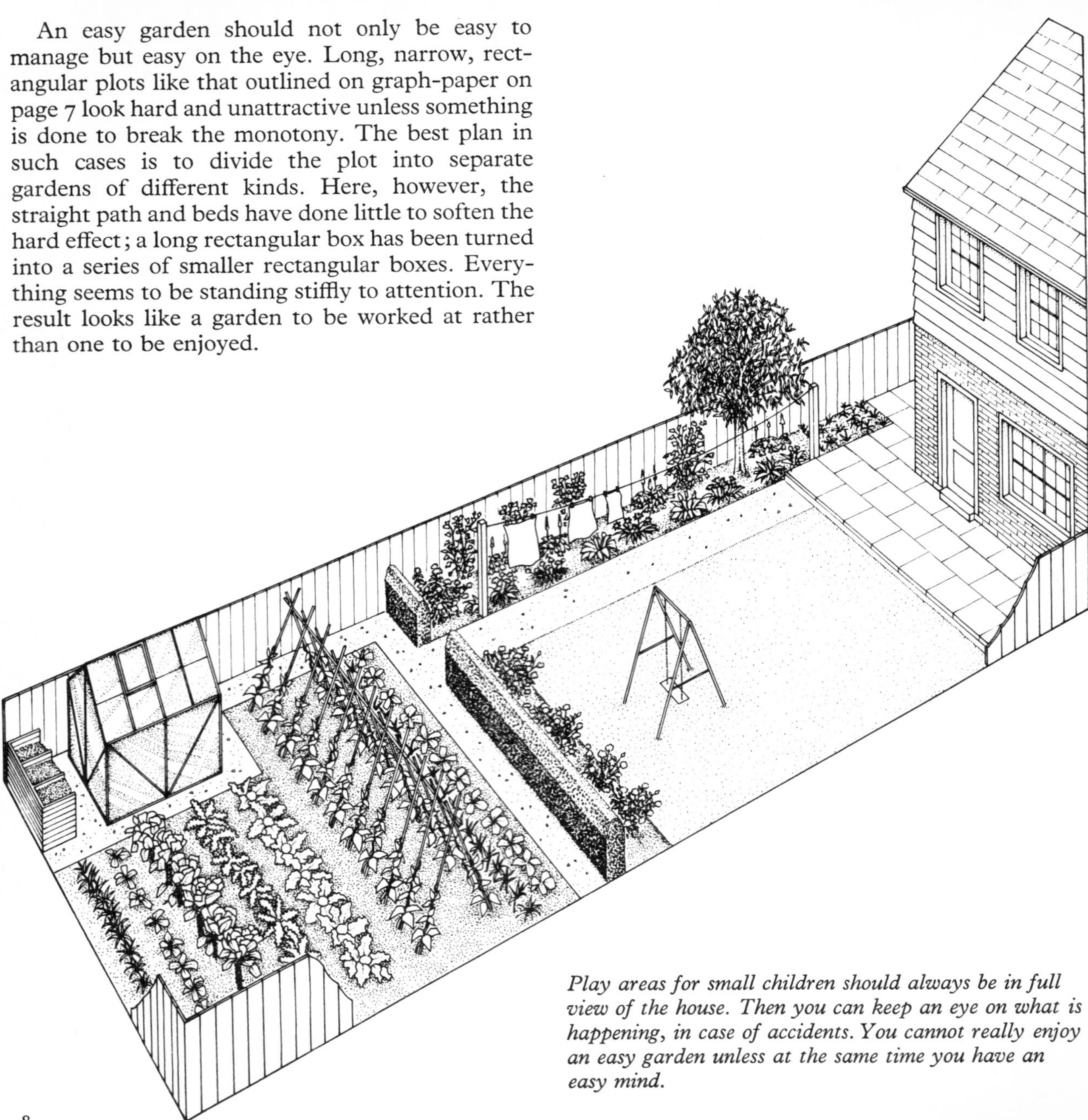

Play areas for small children should always be in full view of the house. Then you can keep an eye on what is happening, in case of accidents. You cannot really enjoy an easy garden unless at the same time you have an easy mind.

The same plot of ground has here been treated in a less formal and more relaxed way. Just as there are no straight lines in nature, so there are none in this garden—except for the terrace or patio, which is really an extension of the house, and the vegetable and fruit gardens, which are more easily managed if the crops are in straight rows. The sloping ground has been changed to different levels, with steps down from the terrace. Curved borders let the plants be seen from different angles and break the garden into separate 'rooms'. Stepping-stones are set flush with the lawn, for easy mowing.

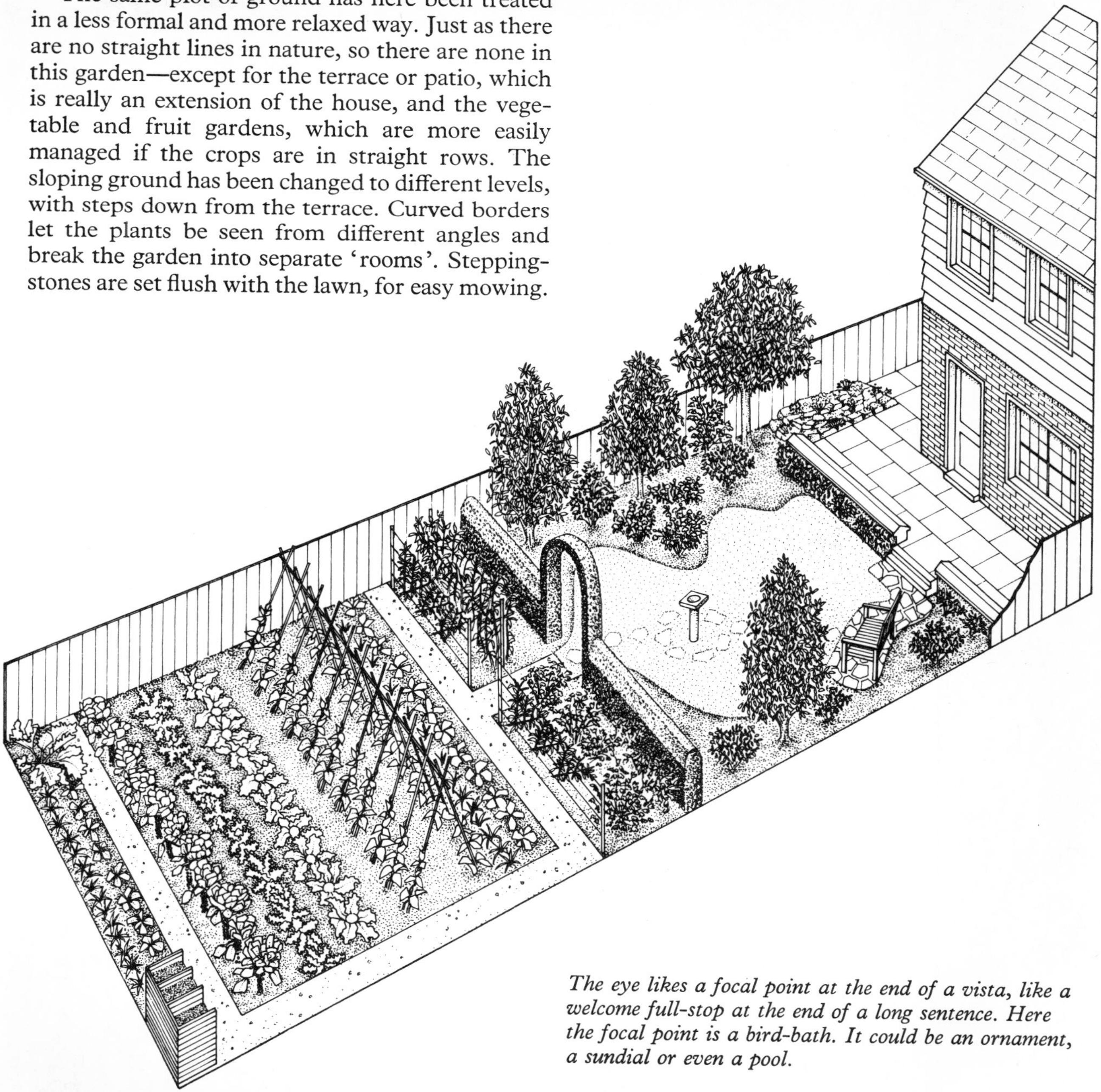

The eye likes a focal point at the end of a vista, like a welcome full-stop at the end of a long sentence. Here the focal point is a bird-bath. It could be an ornament, a sundial or even a pool.

A short, square garden is a common problem, especially in large towns, where land is very valuable. The most important thing is not to include too many features. In a small space they become fussy and restless, like a room with too much furniture in it. So try to cut down the list of things you want to a few essentials. Trees, if any, must be few and small, or they will make the house gloomy. A good way to give a short garden the appearance of length is to turn the axis of the lawn diagonally, and then to emphasise the line of sight with an ornament as focal point.

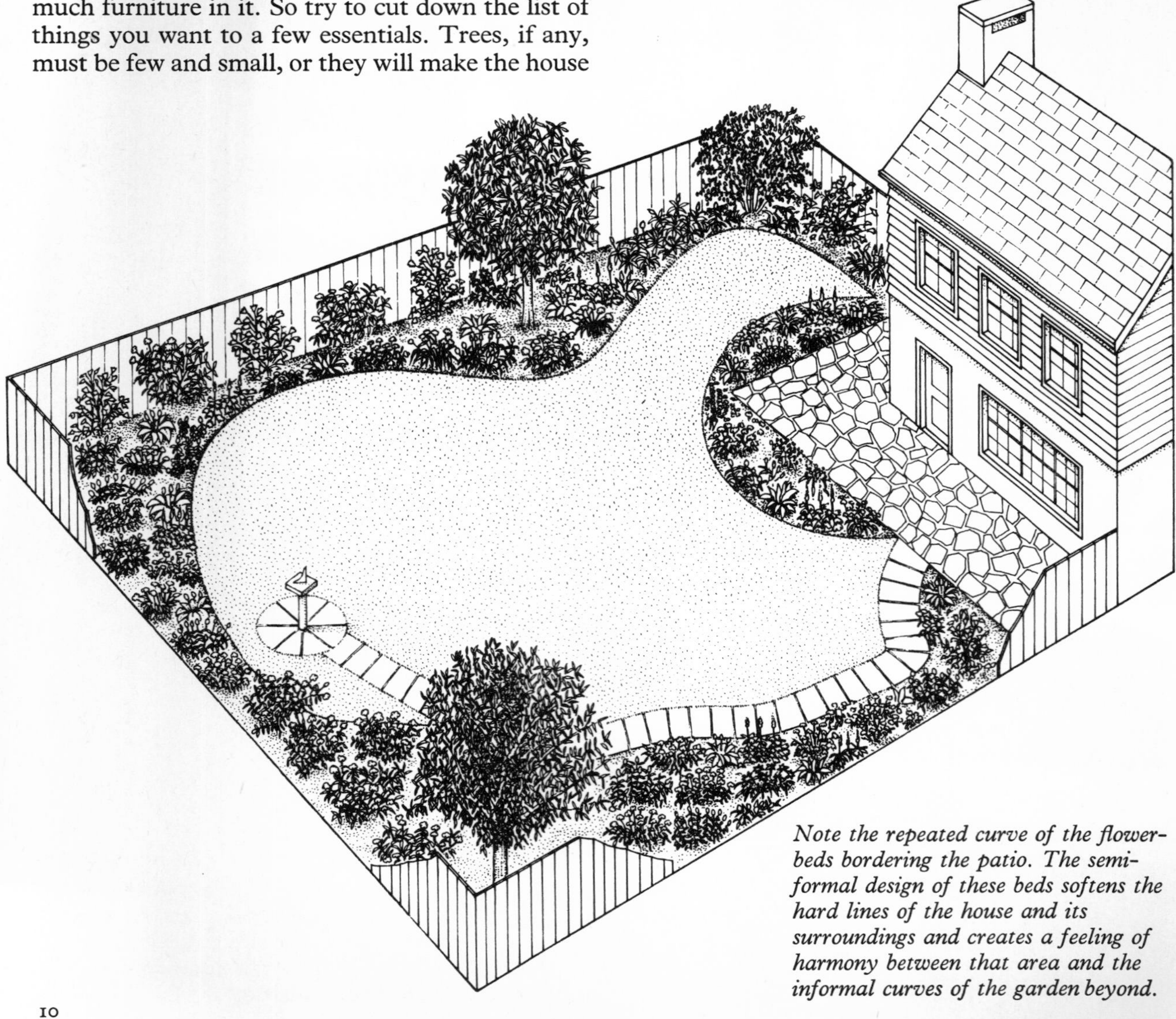

Note the repeated curve of the flower-beds bordering the patio. The semi-formal design of these beds softens the hard lines of the house and its surroundings and creates a feeling of harmony between that area and the informal curves of the garden beyond.

An awkwardly shaped plot which is wider at one end than the other may be divided into different areas as shown here. The main pleasure-garden, consisting of a lawn surrounded by curved borders, is based on a vista from the house terrace, with a weeping tree as focal point. A formal rose-garden backed by rambler roses gives added interest from the house and screens a large vegetable patch. Beyond the lawn and screened by a line of cordon apples is a soft-fruit garden with raspberries, currants and gooseberries. Between the terrace and the lawn are beds for bedding-out plants to give seasonal colour.

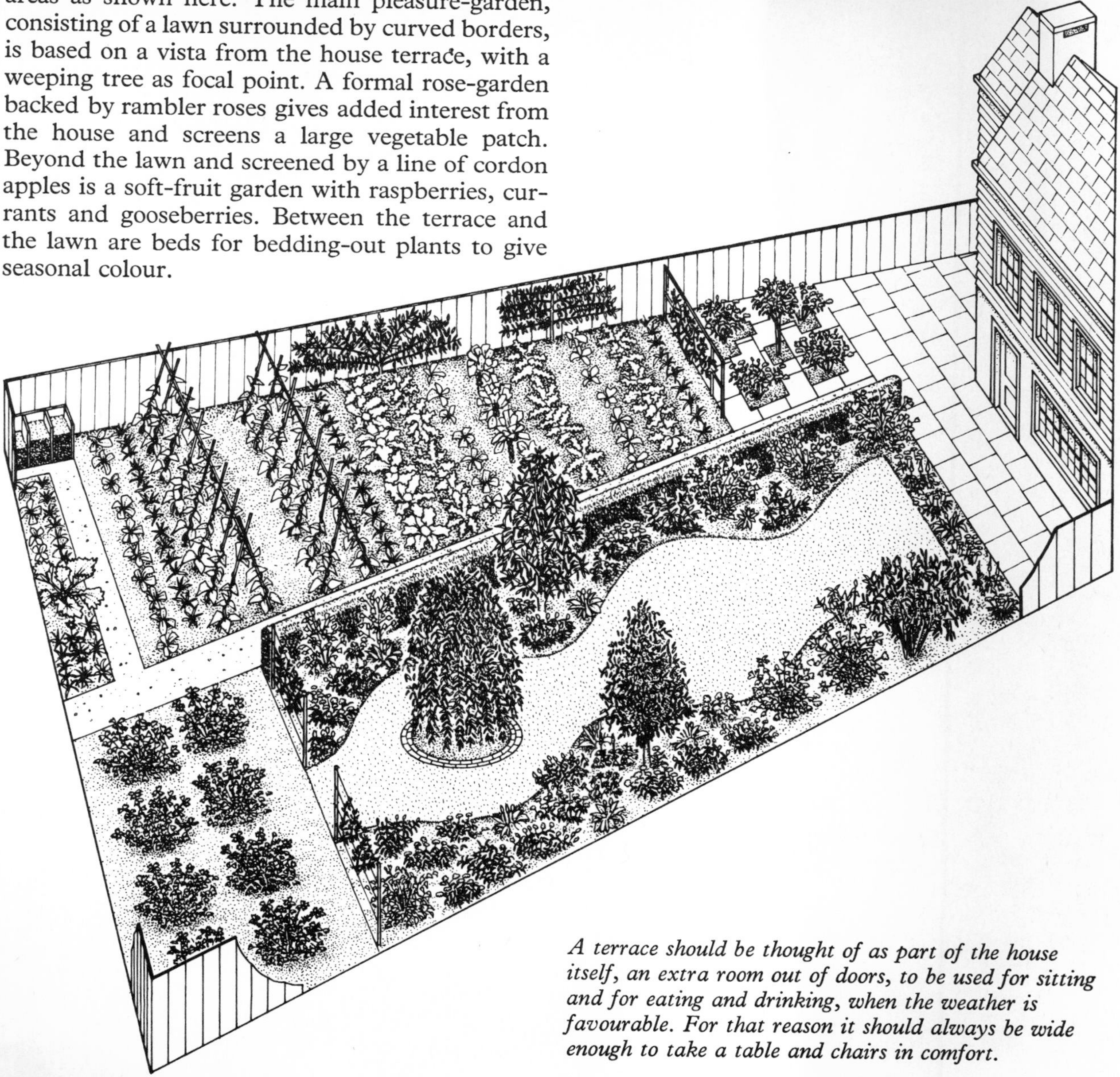

A terrace should be thought of as part of the house itself, an extra room out of doors, to be used for sitting and for eating and drinking, when the weather is favourable. For that reason it should always be wide enough to take a table and chairs in comfort.

Clearing the Site

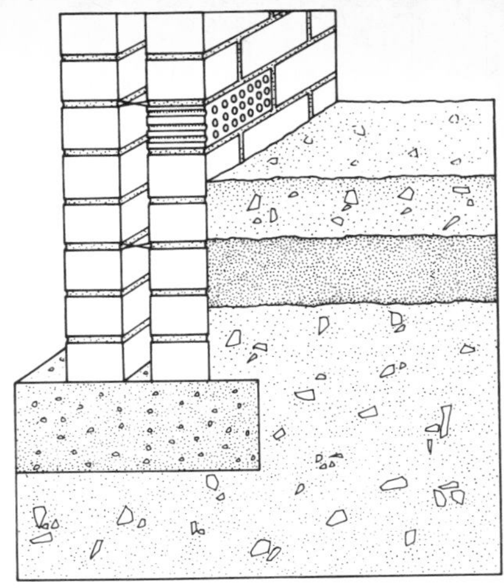

Section through foundations, showing subsoil on top of topsoil

IT TAKES a good deal of imagination to visualise the garden of your dreams when you face the scene of desolation left by the average builder on the plot of land surrounding the new house he has just finished.

The ground is usually covered with an assortment of broken bricks, lumps of plaster, droppings of concrete and mortar, cement, smashed drainpipes and bits of wood. What is to be done with all that rubbish? The answer is simple. *If it will burn, burn it. If it will not burn, use it.*

When you are making your new garden, you are going to need all the hard material you can find, to make a good solid foundation for paths and terraces. So instead of cursing the builder for littering the ground with bits and pieces, bless him for leaving you exactly the sort of stuff you would otherwise have to buy. In fact, if you can manage to have a word with him before he finishes the job, tell him not to bother to clear up; you don't mind doing it for him. You can even suggest that he dumps the rubbish from the next door plot on your ground as well, and you will get rid of it for him. He will probably jump at the offer, and you will have a free supply of just what you need.

Above all, tell the builder not to bother to level the ground but to leave those heaps of soil which were dug out from the foundations of the house just where they are. That will save you a great deal of work later on.

The reason is that subsoil is usually hard, infertile stuff which should be put back where it belongs—underneath the topsoil, not on top of it. *The roots of plants like the layers of soil to remain where nature intended: subsoil below and top soil above.* That is why tidy builders are much worse than untidy ones. Tidy builders, in order to level the site, spread that subsoil all over the ground instead of leaving it in heaps by the places where it was excavated. The result is that it becomes almost impossible ever to put the layers of soil back in their right order again.

It is quite easy, though, to shift a mound of excavated subsoil—or get someone else to shift it for you—to a suitable part of your site, ready to be used where necessary to build up different levels in your garden; the topsoil will, of course, first be removed from such places and later replaced over the built-up subsoil.

If you have planned out your garden in advance, as described in the previous section, you will be able to mark out the paths and remove the topsoil from them to a spade's depth before you start moving the bits of brick and other hard rubble: then you can put the rubble directly in place and so save yourself the effort of having to move it twice. (The removed topsoil can be added to borders or vegetable and fruit gardens, which it will deepen and enrich.)

Make sure when clearing up builder's rubble round the house that nothing is left that will interfere with the efficiency of the building itself. There may be airbricks, which are those perforated ones set in the lower part of the brickwork. They are intended for ventilation, to allow a free current of air and so prevent the very serious troubles that can arise in a building subject to damp and airless conditions. It is therefore absolutely vital that those airbricks should not be obstructed in any way. So see that there are no bits of brick or anything else blocking up the air inlets; bricklayers are not always as careful as they ought to be to see that the holes are not covered with drippings of mortar. There should also be a clear two courses of brickwork between the airbrick and the ground level, so that soil does not get into the holes.

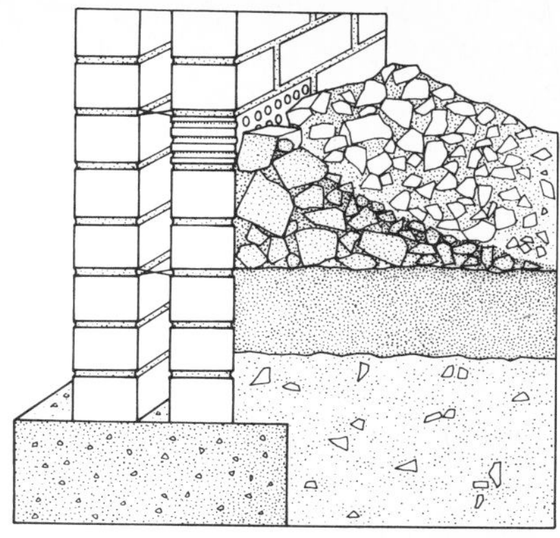

Airbrick partly obscured by mortar rubble

It is particularly important to be careful about such things if you decide to have plants in a bed next to the house itself. Nothing can look nicer than a shrub or climber against the wall, but it is all too easy when planting or weeding to throw earth about without noticing. Take care never to let earth come above the level of the damp-proof course in the wall, or you may damage the structure of your house permanently. Once damp has been allowed to get into the walls it can be very difficult to cure.

So much for the man-made rubbish that has to be cleared from the site before you can start to make your garden. In addition, there will most likely be a great deal of natural rubbish in the form of weeds, which can be much more difficult to conquer. After all, even the biggest pile of broken bricks or displaced subsoil does not grow any bigger, but the natural undergrowth does at a frightening rate unless something is done to check it. Even if the ground was pasture land before it was split up into separate building plots, it is likely that, during the many months the house has taken to build, the grass has grown waist-high and been invaded by coarse weeds until it has become a jungle.

To start with the biggest problems, there may be an old tree on the site. If it is in good condition and pleasant to look at, the best thing may be to leave it alone, make a feature of it and build the garden round it. That will certainly give you a much quicker result than if you plant new young trees, which may take so many years to reach a good size that only your children, or even your grandchildren, will be able to enjoy them in their full beauty.

On the other hand, a great many tall native trees that have been there for a long time are not really suited to a small garden. They may look splendid in the middle of a large field, but they can totally dwarf the average sized plot and throw so much shade that the garden becomes a gloomy instead of a bright and colourful place, and sun-loving plants will not grow successfully in it.

Really large trees should be removed by experts, who will have the correct equipment to make sure the tree falls in the right direction instead of on the house. It is best if the roots are removed from the ground, but if that is not possible—or if, as often happens, the builder has already had the tree chopped down and left a large stump—the roots should be killed before they have a chance to throw up new shoots. A simple way to do this is to bore several large holes in the stump and fill them with saltpetre or sodium chlorate. In a few months the chemicals will have impregnated the stump and made it easy to burn with a bonfire built on it.

Weed-killer being poured into holes bored into tree-stump

Smaller trees can be pulled bodily out of the ground, roots and all, by means of a device known as a monkey-jack. A notch is cut in the trunk of the tree and the spear of the jack is stuck into it. The base of the jack is stood firmly in the ground to one side of the tree, the long handle is moved up and down, and the roots are pulled up as easily as a car-jack lifts the wheels off the ground.

Brambles and other thorny undergrowth can wound you severely when you set about clearing them; the vicious spines have a nasty habit of breaking off and remaining in your flesh as a painful reminder for weeks, resisting all attempts to dig them out with a needle. So when you tackle such clearing jobs always put on old clothes which you do not mind getting torn. Wear a pair of the stoutest gloves you can find and knee-length, or better still thigh-length, rubber boots to protect your legs. Armoured in this way you can cut down all that prickly undergrowth without injury; cut it right down to ground level and stack it for three or four months, by which time it should be dry enough to make a spectacular bonfire.

When all the top growth has been removed, the roots can be dug up, put to dry with the rest, and added to the bonfire. If you find the roots hard to dig up with a spade, borrow or hire a mattock, which you swing like a pickaxe but which has a broad blade capable of chopping through almost anything.

If you do not have the time or the energy or the wish to do this clearing work yourself, you can always hire a contractor with a powered machine to do the job for you. So long as you make it clear to him exactly what you want (this is where that plan on paper comes in handy, to save later arguments on what he was told to do), he can bulldoze that ground into shape in a few hours, altering the levels to suit your requirements. The price, which should be fixed before he starts, will not be anything like as high as the expense of your own time and labour if you were to count up the hours the job would take you to do by hand and cost them at a normal hourly rate.

Tree being torn up by monkey jack

The Soil

A LITTLE thought given to your soil at the start will make your gardening much easier.

There are six basic types of soil: stony, clayey, sandy, limy, peaty and loamy. Dig out a few spadefuls of earth and see which of those types you have. Nearly all soil began as solid rock, which in the course of time split into particles of different sizes. The nature of the original rock and the size of the particles to which the weather has reduced it determine the kind of soil in your garden.

Stony soil

Stony soil is the hardest to deal with. It is young soil, and can be rather stubborn. The action of weather on the rock has not gone very far, so the proportion of soil to rock is rather low. The bad thing about stony soil is the effort it needs. The good thing about it is that it is usually well drained.

Clayey soil

Clayey soil is at the other extreme. It is very old soil. The particles of rock have become so finely ground over the years that they have reached a state which scientists call colloidal and gardeners call sticky. In wet weather clay soils cling to the spade; in dry weather they set as hard as concrete. Generally they are pasty looking, and range in colour from grey to yellowish. The bad thing about clay is that it is hard to work. The good thing about it is its very high potential fertility.

Sandy soil

Sandy soil is midway between stone and clay. It is middle-aged soil. The particles have been broken down more than those of stony soil but not as much as those of clay. They are usually light in colour as well as texture. The bad thing about sandy soil is that it fails to hold moisture and plant foods. The good thing about it is that it is easy to work.

Limy soil

Limy soil is of two kinds: shallow, with more or less solid chalk below, and deeper, with the chalk or lime mixed with other material; so there are various kinds of limy soil, ranging from light ones to heavy mixtures of chalk and clay. The bad thing about limy soils is that some plants simply refuse to grow in them at all. The good thing is that they never become sour from too much acid.

Peaty soil

Peaty soil is old and fossilised. It is full of remains of dead plants

Stony soil

Sandy soil

Clayey soil

Peaty soil

which have been preserved from decay by acid conditions, just as pickles are preserved by vinegar, and may be found where the garden was once heathland. It is dark in colour, sometimes almost black. The bad thing about it is that it is usually very acid. The good thing about it is that it holds water like a sponge if correctly managed.

Loamy soil

Loamy soil is the ideal kind for most garden purposes. It contains a well-balanced mixture of clay and organic matter. Usually it is a rich brown colour. There are no bad things about loam—only good ones—though some loams are better than others.

Loamy soil

WAYS TO IMPROVE SOIL

Try to look at soil from the plant's point of view. To be comfortable and happy, plants need soil that is sweet, allows the roots to breathe, and contains the right amount of food.

Sweetening

If a soil is too acid it is said to be sour. To see if yours is all right, measure its acidity by means of a small soiltesting kit, which can be bought quite cheaply. Take samples of soil, shake them up with water and add a few drops of the indicator solution. This will change colour according to the soil's pH, which is a measure of its acidity. A pH of 7 is neutral; higher figures show that the soil is alkaline; lower figures mean it is acid. Most plants grow best in a slightly acid soil with a pH of about 6·5. If your soil is more acid that than, add lime to sweeten it. The best form for garden use is ground chalk (calcium carbonate), which does not harm leaves if it touches them. The amount needed to reduce acidity to the right level depends not only on the pH but also on the nature of the soil, as shown below.

Chalk needed to sweeten soil (per square yard/square metre)

Present pH:	6·0	5·5	5·0	4·5	4·0
Acidity:	slight	moderate	marked	strong	very strong
	lb/kg	lb/kg	lb/kg	lb/kg	lb/kg
Stony/sandy soil	½/·25	1 / ·45	1½/ ·70	2/ ·90	2½/1·15
Loamy soil	¾/·35	1½/ ·70	2¼/1·00	3/1·35	4 /1·80
Clayey soil	1 /·45	2 / ·90	3 /1·35	4/1·80	5 /2·25
Peaty soil	1¼/·60	2½/1·15	3¾/1·70	5/2·25	6 /2·75

Note: If hydrated lime is used instead of chalk, apply at half the above rates.

Be careful not to over-lime your soil. The right quantity of lime releases suitable amounts of plant foods that sour soils lock up; but too much lime may release such large amounts that they poison some plants.

To complicate matters, some other important foods are made unavailable to certain plants by the presence of lime. This applies particularly to iron, which some plants, known as lime-haters, are quite unable to take up from limy soil; so they become iron-starved, their leaves turn yellow and they weaken and die. A list of such plants appears later in this book in the section *Lime-haters*. Sadly, they include some very beautiful things such as rhododendrons and most of the heathers. It is possible to grow these in limy soil nowadays by feeding them with modern chemicals containing iron in chelated form, which is not affected by lime; but you have to keep repeating the dose regularly to prevent the plants from dying. That is not gardening the easy way, but the hard (and expensive) way. So do not try to grow lime-haters in limy ground. There are plenty of lime-lovers, which will do much better without any effort on your part.

Digging with knees bent

Cultivating

The next thing to consider about the soil is its physical texture. To human beings, the most obvious thing about soil is the colour, size and character of the solid particles. To plant roots, which have to live in it, what matters most about soil is not the solid bits but the spaces between them. On the size of those spaces the whole well-being of the plant depends. In heavy clay the spaces are too small, so neither water and air nor plant roots can penetrate it easily. At the other extreme, in sandy soil the spaces are too big, so moisture quickly disappears and roots shrivel. To make soil as easy as possible, both for the gardener and the plants, it must be turned into something between those extremes. The best way is to dig it. That is quite easy so long as your spade is bright and sharp. A stainless steel one is ideal, because the soil does not cling to it and so the physical effort is greatly reduced. To use as little muscle-power as possible, let the weight of your body do as much of the work as it can. As you slice the spade into the soil, bring your foot down on the shoulder of the spade and lean on it rather than push it; you will find that much less tiring to the arms. Allow your knees to bend instead of keeping them stiff. To avoid hard work, always move soil as short a distance as possible. Stretch a garden line along the middle of the plot so as to divide it into two halves lengthwise. At one end dig out a trench, to one spade's depth and width, half-way across the plot. Pile the earth from this shallow trench next to the other side, which has not been dug, at the same end. Dig a second trench behind the first, throwing the soil from this, upside-down, into the first trench. Continue turning over the soil in this way to the other end of the plot. Fill the last trench on that side with soil from a trench dug across the other side and continue back along the plot, filling in the last trench of all with the pile of soil which you placed beside it at the beginning.

Turning over the soil to one spade's depth in this way is known as single-digging, and that is quite enough for most well-drained soils. Yet a great many gardeners, and gardening books for that matter, insist that the ground should be double-dug, in other words dug to two spade's depths. This involves getting down into each trench as work proceeds and turning over the subsoil with a fork to loosen it. If you are a masochist and enjoy tiring yourself out with unnecessary physical effort, by all means double-dig your ground in this way, but do not expect it to improve your soil; in fact it will be a waste of time with most loams and do more harm than good to chalky, stony and sandy soils.

The only type of soil that needs this hard labour called double-digging is badly drained heavy clay. To find out if your soil comes into this category, dig a hole during wet weather. If the hole fills with water which stands for a long time, that means it cannot drain away properly. In such conditions, breaking up the subsoil by double-digging can improve matters greatly, especially if you dig some gravel or grit into the subsoil. The important thing is to try to stop it from forming a solid mass again. If no gravel or grit is available, a layer of brushwood in the subsoil may help; it will take some time to decay, and will improve the drainage while it lasts.

If you cannot face all that digging by hand, borrow or hire a motor-powered rotary cultivator, which has blades that can turn over the soil of a whole garden in a few hours. It takes no effort except steering.

Trenching and double-digging

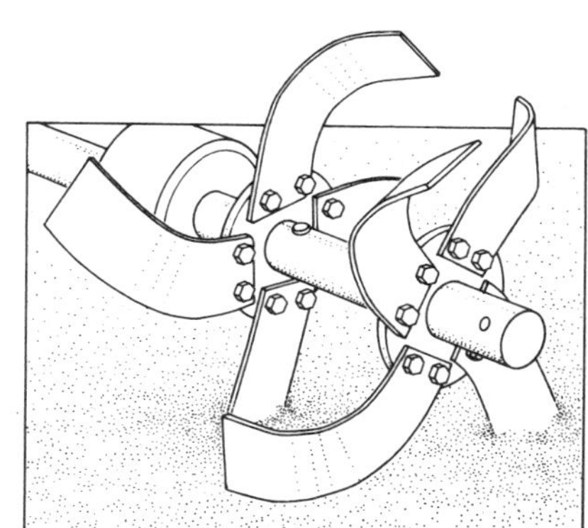

Blades of rotary hoe

Draining

If even double-digging does not succeed in getting rid of water, some more thorough method of draining the soil will be necessary. The most efficient—and expensive—way is to lay a 4-inch (10 cm) drain-pipe 3 feet (about 1 metre) below the surface from one corner of the plot diagonally to the other; it should have a fall of about one in a hundred. The lower end should lead into a ditch, if you are lucky enough to have one bordering your garden, or failing that a soakaway filled with stones, broken bricks, lumps of concrete or any other hard rubble. Branch drains of 3-inch (7·5 cm) pipes, laid 15 feet (4·5 metres) apart, are joined to the main drain at an angle of about 45 degrees, herring-bone fashion. Over the pipes lay a good covering of stones or coarse gravel before filling in the soil; that will keep the drains from getting clogged up with earth.

A cheaper way than using drainpipes, but still quite satisfactory, is to put a 6-inch (15 cm) layer of stones or other hard rubble at the bottom of the drainage trenches. In heavy soils nothing else can ease your life as much as good drainage, because you never again have to face the most muscle-aching job in all gardening—that is, trying to cope with ground that is either as sticky as glue or as hard as iron (which is what ill-drained heavy ground becomes in hot dry weather).

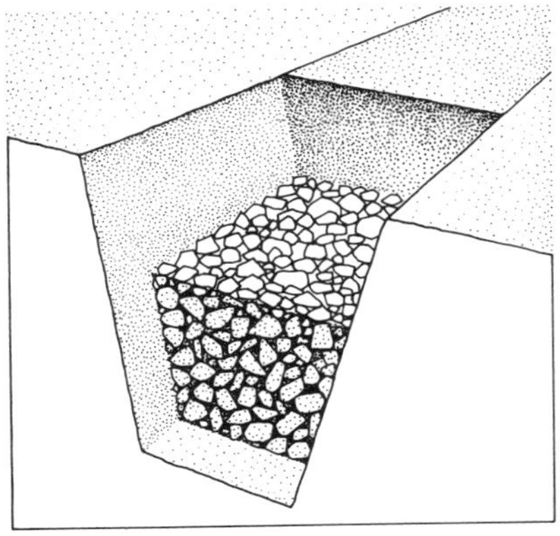

Draining to a soakaway

Manuring

Nearly all soils will benefit greatly from the addition of plenty of organic waste material. Best of all is animal manure, but nowadays that is becoming scarce and expensive. If you are lucky enough to be able to obtain some, you can mix it into the soil during digging, but keep it in the top layer; if buried too deeply it may be below the reach of plant roots, so its goodness will be wasted. Other materials of a bulky, fibrous nature such as peat and well-rotted leaf mould also make the texture of the soil much pleasanter and easier both for the gardener and for the plants. Such materials hold moisture and plant-foods, keep the crumbs of soil from sticking together into a hard mass, and produce a rich, brown substance called humus, which is essential to the health of the soil and everything that lives in it. Every household can have a supply of this organic, humus-forming substance by making compost. Simply save all kitchen waste such as potato-peelings, carrot-tops, tea leaves, and coffee-grounds, mix it with garden waste (leaves, grass-mowings, old flower-heads and the like) and stack it in layers, with a sprinkling of earth between, either in an open compost-heap or in one of the compost bins specially made for the purpose, which greatly speeds up the process. In a few months the waste material will have turned into a rich brown crumbly substance which will greatly benefit the soil. If you have a big enough supply of waste material, an excellent plan is to have an arrangement of three bins: compost material is still being added to the first, the compost in the second is maturing and that in the third is ready for use.

Compost may be dug in, but in the easy garden is best spread on the surface, where it will suppress most weeds and make those that do appear much easier to pull out, because it stops the soil from forming a hard crust.

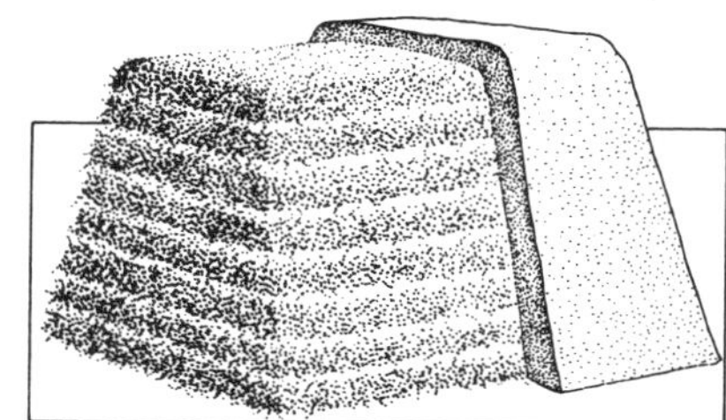

Simple compost heap

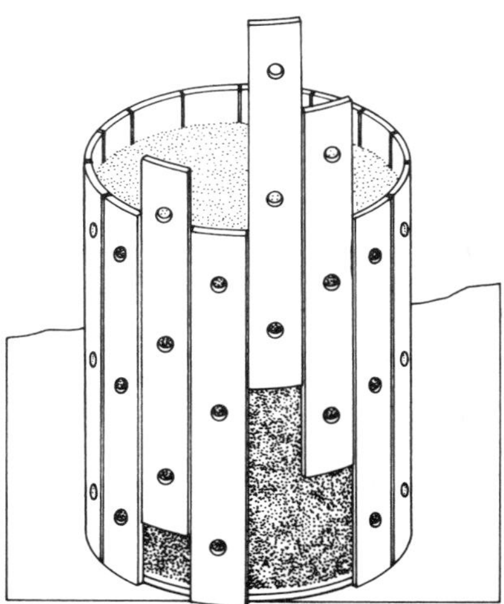

Circular compost container

Construction Jobs

THE EASIEST parts of your garden to look after are—or should be—the paved parts: paths, terrace or patio, and steps. Properly constructed, they should need little, if any, further attention. The more maintenance they require, the less easy is the garden.

Make the first expense the last, whenever you can possibly manage it. That goes not only for expense in terms of money but even more for expense in terms of effort. Never use any paving material that will cause work later on. For that reason we will not even consider such things as gravel, which, no matter how beautiful it may look in other people's gardens, condemns its owner to the drudgery of continual weeding, mending and rolling. The most important thing about a path or terrace is that it should be absolutely firm. It must never shift or sink. And the surface should be weed-free, not become slippery and not be damaged by the weather, particularly frost.

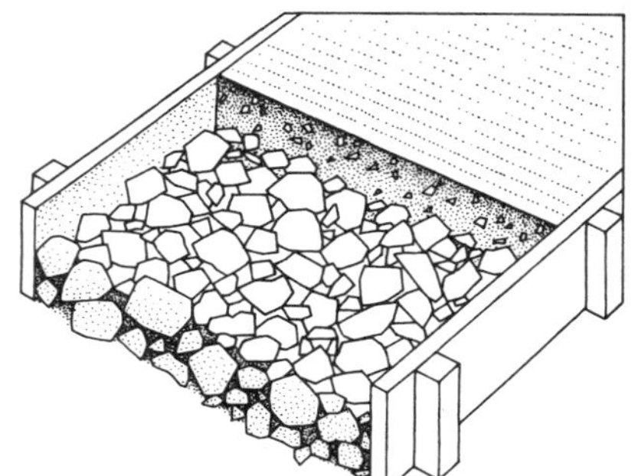

Constructing a concrete path

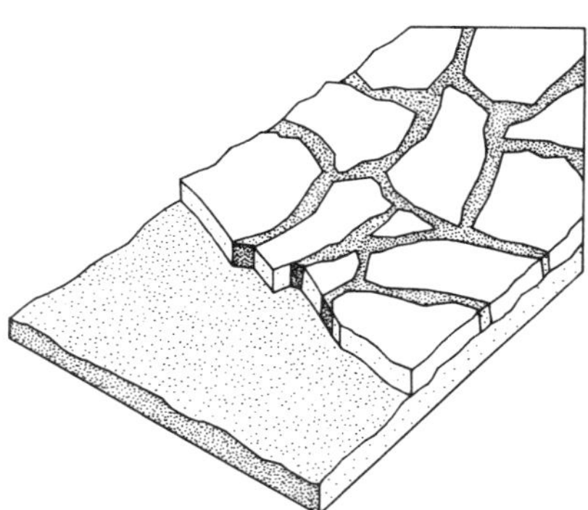

Constructing a crazy-paving path

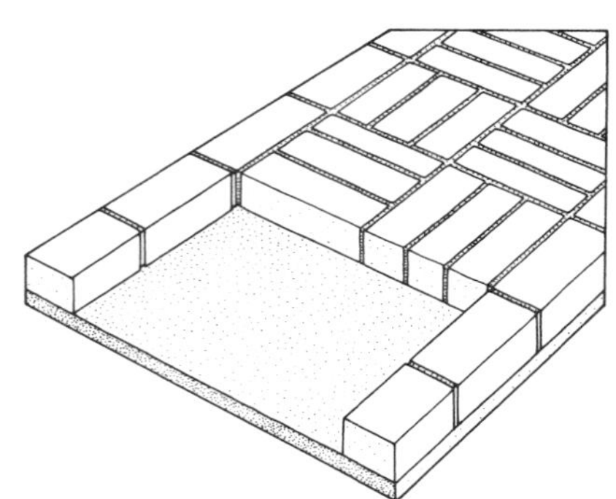

Constructing a brick path

PATHS

Concrete

The easiest and most trouble-free path is one made of concrete. First a firm foundation must be made. Mark out the sides of the path with pegs and cord, then dig the soil out to a depth of 9 inches (*c.* 23 cm) (if it is good topsoil it can be added to beds or borders). Fill the bottom 6 inches (*c.* 15 cm) of the trench so formed with hard rubble, such as broken bricks, or stones, and ram it down. Then lay 3 inches (7·5 cm) of concrete over this in sections in the following way. Peg a long piece of wood at each side of where the path is to be, so that the top edge is 2 inches (5 cm) above the surface of the rubble; make sure by means of a spirit level that the tops of the pieces of wood are level with each other and level along their entire length. Between the lengths of wood, spread concrete made by mixing 1 part of cement, 2 parts of sand and 3 parts of shingle with enough water to make it into a stiff paste, but not sloppy. Finish by smoothing the surface with a piece of board placed across the lengths of wood and moved to and fro as it is drawn from one end of the section to the other. Be very careful not to leave any airholes in the cement. At the end of the section fix a cross-piece of wood cut to the width of the path and level with the side-pieces, and bring the concrete flush with this; any surplus can be thrown into the foundation of the next section. Cover the finished surface with sacking or plastic sheets to stop it from drying out too quickly: the longer it takes to dry the stronger it will be. In three or four days, when the concrete has set, the wood can be moved along and the next section of concrete laid in the same way. If you find the colour of ordinary concrete boring, you can buy a variety of coloured powders which can be mixed with it. Concrete is ideal for utilitarian paths such as in the vegetable garden. Many people find it unattractive in the pleasure garden, particularly near the house. For such places there are much nicer looking materials.

Stone

Slabs of natural stone make beautiful paths, particularly in formal gardens, but they have two snags: they are expensive, and they tend to be irregular in thickness, so that it can be time-consuming and temper-fraying to lay them really firmly.

Precast slabs

These are made of artificial stone in a variety of sizes and colours, and can be used in all kinds of different patterns. They are absolutely uniform in thickness and very easy to lay.

Bricks

These can be laid on edge in all kinds of attractive designs: straight, curved and in herringbone patterns. They give great visual richness, either alone or in combination with other materials such as stone slabs or cobbles.

Crazy paving

This consists of irregular pieces of broken stone, usually 1½ or 2 inches (5 cm) thick, laid together in random fashion. It is popular for informal effects, especially for winding paths. It takes a good deal of time and effort to lay crazy paving properly so that it does not need constant maintenance later on.

Terrace with pockets for trailing plants

TERRACES

These can be constructed from any of the same materials as paths, alone or in combination. Concrete is the least attractive for terraces; the others can be very appealing visually.

Plants for paving

If you want to brighten up a paved area with some low-growing plants between the stones, you must plan for them from the beginning, by leaving pockets of soil for them. Choose plants that do not mind being trodden on; some indeed will reward you by giving off a pleasant scent when bruised in this way. Among the most fragrant are the prostrate thymes, such as *Thymus serpyllum*, which gives tiny pink or white flowers in the summer, a dwarf-growing mint called *Mentha requiennii*, which forms a peppermint-scented carpet studded with minute mauve flowers, and a compact species of spicy marjoram named *Origanum amanum* with deep pink flowers appearing well into the autumn. Many other carpeting plants are suitable, such as dwarf species of *Arenaria*, *Dianthus*, *Geranium* and *Phlox*. Ask your local plant suppliers for recommendations, and accept what they offer rather than ask for rare kinds; they will know what does best in your locality, and the reason why the most popular varieties are the most popular is simply that they do better than the less popular ones.

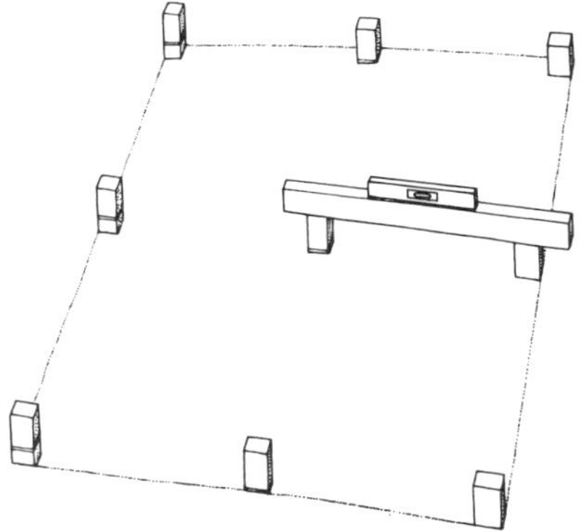

Taking levels

Laying the paving

Apart from pockets of soil to accommodate carpeting plants, there should be no crevices of earth where weeds can grow, otherwise you will have to spend too much time on your knees weeding instead of enjoying yourself. That means that joints in the paving should be filled with cement mortar, through which weeds cannot grow.

The first thing is to make a firm foundation of rubble, as explained under *Paths*. If there is not enough rubble, buy a load of hard-core. To make the job of laying as easy as possible, cover the base with a good layer of sand and make this even by means of a trowel or plasterer's float. To be sure that the surface is level, place a plank of wood on edge along it and put a spirit-level on top of this; sand can then be built up or scooped away as necessary.

Arrange the paving-stones or bricks on top of this sand in a pattern that pleases you. Then, working from the end at which you started, lift out the first piece of paving, spread half an inch of mortar (made up of 4 parts of sand, 1 part cement and water as necessary) over the surface of the sand, replace the piece of paving and tap it firmly into position. Continue with the next piece and work your way along the whole area to be paved till it is finished. Do *not* push the slabs or bricks right against each other, but leave spaces about half an inch wide between them. This not only makes laying much easier but allows more mortar to be worked into these spaces; finish this mortar flush with the top of the paving, wiping any surplus away with a brush or wet cloth so as not to spoil the surface.

This will make absolutely firm paving that will never need weeding (except perhaps occasionally around the carpeting plants) and requires no further maintenance. The reason why paths and terraces should be level is that the force of gravity is then your ally, acting to keep things stable and so make gardening easier. With sloping places, gravity is against you, as you will know if you have ever pushed a mower up a sloping lawn, or tried to stop it from dragging you down. If your plot of ground does slope, the best plan is to turn it into a series of level places. First you will have to find just how much it slopes and in what directions, and for this you need some accurate way of measuring levels. A simple method uses only a spirit level, a long plank and some wooden pegs. At the highest point of your land, bang in a peg until its top is three inches above ground level. Rest one end of the plank on this and the other end on another peg driven into the ground far enough to make the top edge of the plank perfectly level, as shown by the bubble in the spirit-level. The difference between the heights of the two pegs will give you the difference in levels. Further points are measured in the same way so that you can plan what needs to be dug out and what filled in to create the series of level places you want. As we saw in *Clearing the site*, topsoil must still be on top and subsoil beneath when the earth-shifting is finished.

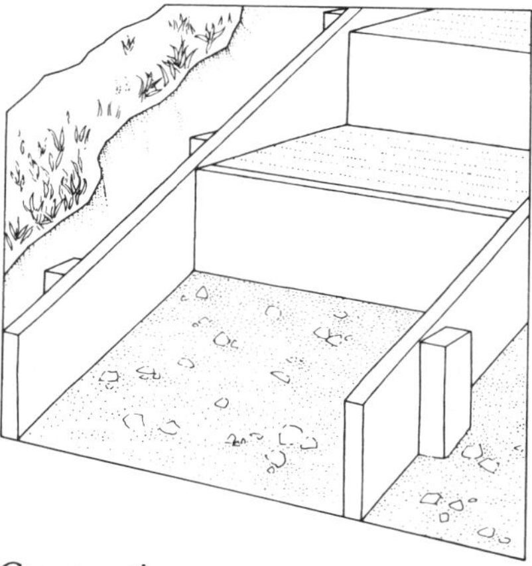

Constructing concrete steps

STEPS

To get from one level to another you will need steps. These can be made of stone slabs or bricks, laid on firm foundations as explained for *Paths* and *Terraces*. They should be wide enough for two people to walk down them side by side, and each step should not be more than 5 inches (13 cm) high or less than 16 inches (*c.* 41 cm) from back to front. Many people slope each step very slightly downwards from front to back; they say that this makes for greater strength and less wear.

Brick and concrete slab steps

RETAINING WALLS

Where there is a marked difference in level between one part of the garden and another, an easy and attractive way to deal with it is to build a retaining wall of stonework. Perhaps the most trouble-free and permanent way of doing this is to set the stones in cement mortar, so that they cannot shift and no weeds can grow between them. That will, however, look rather bare and grim; besides, you will have missed the chance of growing some of the very attractive plants that are particularly suited to walls and look at their best sprouting from crevices and cascading over the stones. If you decide to build your retaining wall without mortar so that it will grow plants ('dry-walling', this is called), the principle of construction is quite simple. Because the weight of earth that has to be held in place is very great, especially after rain, the wall must never be vertical or it may collapse and topple forwards. It must therefore be built with a decided backward slope from the base to the top. Start by digging out a trench about 9 inches (23 cm) deep and somewhat wider than the blocks of stone to be used in building the wall. Half fill this trench with stones or other hard rubble and ram it down very thoroughly, making the back come rather lower than the front. This will ensure that when you lay the first layer of stones they start with a tilt in the right direction. Cover this layer with an inch or so of soil, then add another course of stones, arranged so that the joints between them come above the middles of the stones in the first layer; this will make a much stronger job than if the joints came vertically above each other. Finish with a layer of stones rather wider than the rest from back to front; this will throw rain well back into the earth instead of letting it run down just behind the wall where it might wash away the soil and weaken the whole structure.

Dry stone retaining wall

Among the many plants that will flourish in dry walls are species of *Alchemilla*, *Alyssum*, *Androsace*, *Arabis*, *Armeria*, *Aubrieta*, *Campanula*, *Dianthus*, *Erodium*, *Iberis*, *Phlox*, *Primula*, *Saxifrage*, *Sedum* and *Sempervivum*. Ask for suitable plants at your local garden centre, where you can see them growing and choose what you fancy.

ROCK GARDENS

More gradual slopes from one level to another can be made into rock gardens. Or if your ground is naturally level and you would like a difference in contour to make a point of interest in an otherwise rather flat scene, you can create an artificial mound of soil with slabs of stone embedded in it where you can grow alpine plants which enjoy, or at any rate look better in, such surroundings. The best types of rock for such purposes are sandstone or limestone. They can be rather expensive if you live a long way from a quarry; and the cost of delivering them from a distance can be more than that of the stone itself. You do not, however, need a great deal; many gardeners overdo things by buying far too much, piling it into a sort of jagged pyramid, and so achieving at colossal expense a very unnatural and unpleasing effect.

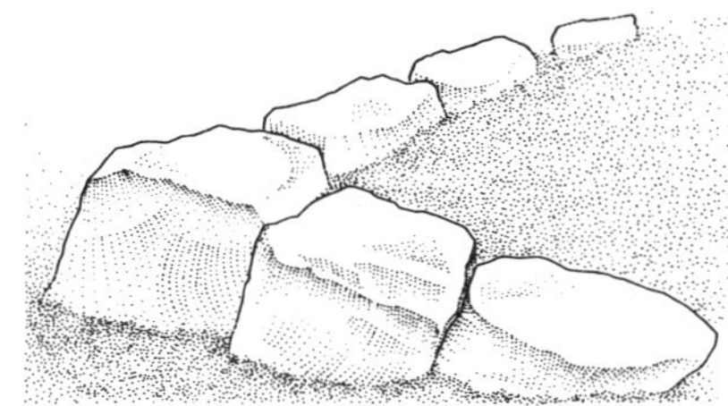

Basic rock garden

Adding to the basic rock garden

All that is needed is enough stone to give the effect of a few rocky outcrops between layers of soil. Start by placing the biggest rock at the corner, tilting it slightly backwards. From that, continue a line of progressively smaller rocks tilted in the same direction, the last one being half buried in the earth. Then place a similar line at right angles to the first. If you have enough rocks you can build another layer further up the slope, and perhaps a third, taking care to make them all tilt in the same direction as if they were part of the same underlying rock formation. Fill in between the rock strata with free-draining soil; if it is at all heavy, mix in plenty of coarse sand or grit. There is an almost unlimited variety of plants to choose from for your rock garden, ranging from small upright shrubs and conifers to creeping plants that cascade over the rocks, and from bright-flowered rock-roses (*Helianthemum*) to the succulent rosette forming plants such as stonecrops (*Sedum*) and house leeks (*Sempervivum*). Once again visit your local garden centre, where you can see them growing, and take your pick.

Screens and Hedges

SCREENS

To enclose the whole of your garden, and those individual parts that you want to keep separate, some sort of screen is essential. It can either be a dead one, such as a fence, or a living one, in the form of a hedge. There is no doubt about the fact that, as far as easy gardening is concerned, the dead boundary has every advantage over the living one. A fence needs no clipping or pruning; it has no roots to rob the border next to it of moisture and nourishment; it does not suffer from diseases or pests, except perhaps woodworm—and not even that if it has been treated thoroughly with preservative.

Your garden probably already has a boundary fence, which was there when you took it over; if so, there is not much you can do about it. The ordinary boarded fence fixed to posts and rails is perfectly serviceable and trouble-free, particularly if the posts are impregnated at the base with an anti-rot liquid and/or bedded in concrete. If you find such a fence unattractive, its look can be softened by training a climbing rose or two up it (see *Roses*) and perhaps a climber or two such as clematis or honeysuckle (see *Climbers*). The trouble is that to save cost boarded fences are often not high enough to protect against wind, and inquisitive neighbours, especially near the house when you want to sit or lie and sunbathe on the terrace. For such places, and for others where there is no existing fence where you need one, there are some ready-made screens obtainable. These are probably the cheapest. They are available in several heights and usually in six-foot lengths. The vertical posts—of chestnut or similar wood—should be stood in creosote or other preservative for a day or two till they have drunk their fill. Choose a calm day to put the hurdles in position, when the weather forecast promises no wind for the next few days, and set the posts firmly in concrete. When this has hardened, the hurdles should be able to stand up to high winds without being loosened, or even blown down. Remember that a screen of this kind can present as much wind-resistance as a ship in full sail. Properly erected wattle hurdles should last for ten years or more.

Interlap woven panels

These are dearer to buy but longer lasting. They are made in various woods, of which one of the best is cedar. Best of all is oak or some similar hardwood, which though the most expensive lasts the longest.

Vertical weatherboard fencing

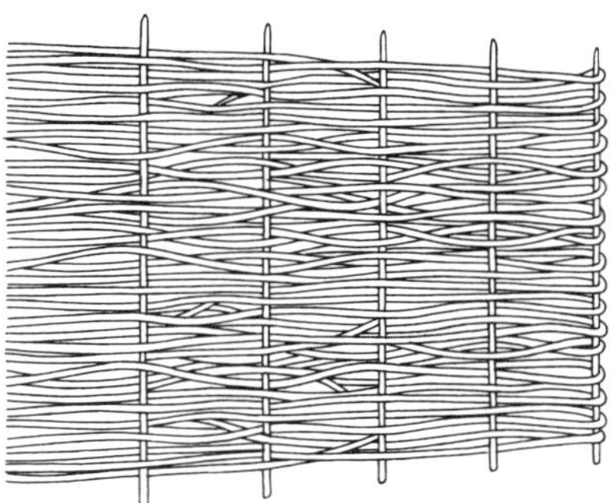

Wattle fencing

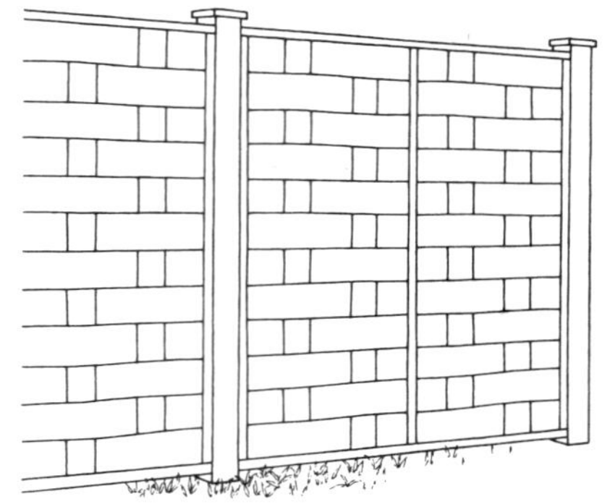

Interwoven panel fencing

Brick walls

The old-fashioned garden was often enclosed in a high brick wall all round, which soaked up the sun and provided a warm place for wall-shrubs and climbers that would be too tender for open ground. It was also perfect for grape vines, espalier pears, and fan-trained peaches and nectarines. Nowadays such brick walls would be prohibitively expensive and in any case would be rather out of place in the average small back garden. However, a low brick wall with a gate in it dividing the front garden from the street is a very practical proposition and often goes with the house, having been built at the same time and with the same type of brick, so that it tones in nicely. To add height, a privet hedge is often planted just inside the wall, but since this will need clipping at least twice a year to keep it tidy, it hardly makes for easy gardening. Besides it has a closed, unwelcoming look. There are easier and pleasanter things available, as we shall see under *Hedges*.

Perforated cement wall panels

Perforated screen blocks

There are many attractive modern artificial-stone blocks of open-work design which are made by pouring a cement-based compound into moulds. These can be laid in mortar, just like brickwork only much more quickly and easily, to make delightful see-through screens which are much more inviting than solid walls. You will find several different patterns of these perforated blocks to choose from at any good garden centre. They are usually fixed to a solid low wall of brickwork or stone to provide a strong base and avoid accidental damage from a carelessly pushed wheelbarrow or children's bicycle.

So long as they are laid on a firm, level foundation and you use a plumb-line (a piece of string with a weight on the end) to make sure they are built vertically, walls made of these perforated slabs can be as high as you like. Or they can be dwarf walls to divide a terrace from a bed on a lower level.

HEDGES

Easy hedges are those that take the least amount of work. Since most of the work involved in hedges consists of clipping and trimming, the easy garden should have only those hedges (if it has hedges at all) that need the least clipping. And since the faster a hedge grows the more it needs clipping, we are faced with one blinding and inescapable truth: *easy hedges are slow-growing hedges.*

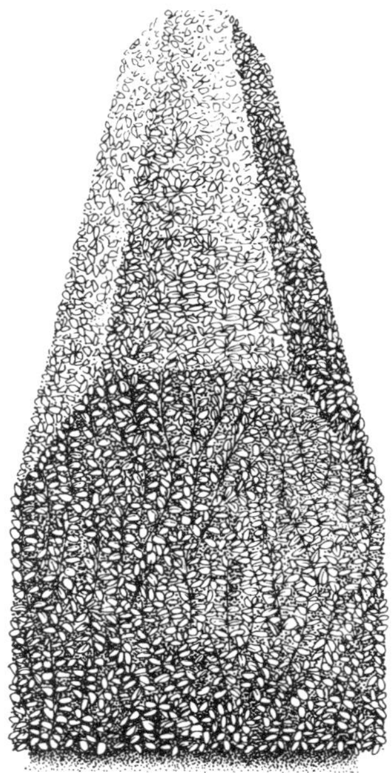
Shaping a hedge

You therefore have to make a choice. Do you want a hedge that will grow as quickly as possible, so as to give shelter from wind, hide an eyesore, or give you a sense of privacy and shut out the prying glances of neighbours? Or do you want a hedge that will take as little looking after as possible? Unfortunately you cannot have both these things together, because they are opposites. You have to decide on one or the other.

To begin with we will take the first of these two extremes, the fast-growing hedge that will do a cover-up job as rapidly as possible. The obvious choice here is an evergreen, since you do not want to be able to see through it at any time of the year.

Privet (*Ligustrum ovalifolium*)
Probably the most commonly planted, and can be obtained in green-leaved and golden varieties; it grows fast, needs clipping two or three times a year, and has hungry, spreading roots which need to be chopped back regularly with a spade if the hedge is next to a border, to prevent them from robbing the soil of all its nourishment for other plants.

Cypresses
These include some of the fastest-growing of evergreens. *Chamaecyparis lawsoniana* is good, and has many varieties with green, blue-grey and golden foliage. Quickest of all is the modern hybrid × *Cupressocyparis leylandii*, which makes a dense screen very rapidly, and can reach a height of thirty feet in a few years. It really wants to be a tree, and it will need clipping several times a year to keep it a hedge instead.

Chinese Honeysuckle (*Lonicera nitida*)
The cheapest evergreen to buy, and does not grow so tall; 5 feet (*c.* 1·50 m) is the limit if it is not to become leggy. But it needs constant trimming throughout the summer to keep it from getting ragged. Evergreen hedges should never be trimmed to a flat top, or they will run the risk of being squashed out of shape by snow, or even hail or heavy rain. Always taper them to a rounded point, which looks nicer in any case.

So much for the rapid growers that need so much hard work to keep them in shape. Now let us look at the easy hedges, which because they grow slowly need the least trimming.

Yew (*Taxus baccata*)
One of the noblest and best. It keeps its shape well, can be grown to

any height you please, from a tall boundary hedge to a dwarf one between different parts of the garden, and needs only one trimming a year.

Holly (*Ilex aquifolium*)
Another excellent slow-grower which makes a dense, impenetrable hedge. Besides the usual green kind there are attractive varieties with silver-edged and gold-edged leaves. Since male and female plants are separate, some of each sex should be grown if you want berries.

Box (*Buxus sempervirens*)
Perhaps the slowest-growing of all, so if you plant it to provide shelter you will have to wait several years for it to do so. When it is full-grown, however, it makes the most trouble-free hedge and needs less clipping than any other.

Flowering Hedges
There are several kinds of plant that combine usefulness as a hedge with beauty of flower. They need only light trimming, otherwise you will cut away the flower-buds. Roses (*Rosa* species) of various kinds are excellent, as are species and hybrids of *Escallonia* and *Berberis*, particularly *Berberis* × *stenophylla*, which has vicious spines and honey-scented golden flowers.

Dwarf hedges
For edgings to beds, especially in formal parts of the garden, dwarf hedges of suitable plants look very attractive. Varieties of Lavender (*Lavandula* species) are very beautiful with their sweet-scented, bee-laden flowers; but make sure you get a really dwarf kind, since some sorts grow leggy. Rosemary (*Rosmarinus officinalis*) is very pretty. Rue (*Ruta graveolens*) with blue-grey foliage, and Cotton lavender (*Santolina chamaecyparissus*) with grey, aromatic leaves, are two other suitable kinds. These dwarf hedges take a certain amount of clipping and removal of dead flower-heads, but it is very light work and quite restful.

Planting distances for hedges vary considerably, not only between species but even between varieties of the same species. So when you buy your plants ask the supplier how far apart they should be to make a good hedge.

Leylandii hedge

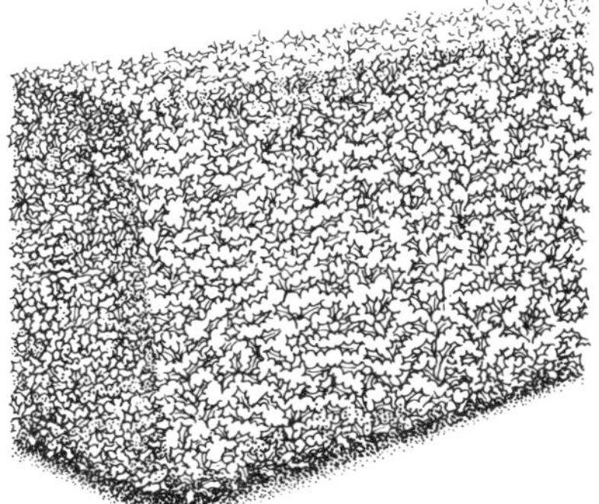

Holly hedge

Trees and Shrubs

THE EASIEST growing things in the easy garden, that is to say those which need the least labour, are the trees and shrubs. Or rather they should need the least labour if you plant the right kinds. If you do not, they can give endless trouble.

Mutilated tree caused by planting too big a kind

TREES

Since trees are the permanent features of the garden, and if all goes well you are going to live with them for a long time, they need to be chosen with great care. The most important things to remember are these: *never plant kinds that will grow too big, never plant too many, and never plant them too close together.*

It is quite difficult when buying a young sapling from your nursery or garden-centre to realise how quickly it is going to grow. Before purchase always ask how tall it will become and how far its branches will spread. The best labour-saving device is a little imagination. With your graph-paper plan and a ruler to help you, try to imagine what the garden will look like in ten years' time when the trees have grown, and how it will appear by the time they have reached full size. If you find this difficult, a good way to aid your imagination is to mark on your plan the position of each tree you are thinking of planting and draw round it a circle, to scale, representing the spread of its branches when it is fully grown. Make sure those circles do not touch the house or overlap each other at any point. That will stop you from making the mistake of planting big trees such as oaks or limes or plane-trees which, however noble they may look in parkland, are quite unsuitable for a small garden. Quite apart from the needless labour involved, it is a crime against nature to have to cut off the limbs of wide-spreading trees simply because they are stretching them out as they were intended to do. Such horrible mutilated stumps of branches as shown here, the result of continual lopping to keep the tree within a confined space, are all too common a sight in gardens and streets. Yet there is really no excuse for such butchery; a little thought and imagination, a touch of sympathy for the victims, would have prevented misplaced giants from being planted in the first place.

There are many small trees that are much more suitable for the average garden and can be relied upon to keep within bounds without having to have their heads or arms cut off. Some of the neatest and most compact are to be found among the Japanese Maples, which never need pruning and are self-shaping. They grow as if someone had drawn an invisible line round them beyond which the branches are not allowed to go; so they never become untidy. One of these self-shaping Japanese Maples is shown here, but there are several other kinds to be found at any good tree nursery or garden centre. It is important for easy gardening never to plant trees too close together. To calculate how far apart trees should be planted, a good rule is this. Find out how far across each tree will spread when it is full-grown. Add these two figures together and divide the result by two. That will give you the least distance that there should be between the trees to make sure that they never get in each other's way.

Small Japanese maple tree

The next thing to consider is the purpose of the tree. Is it to provide shade or shelter from the wind? If so, make sure that it is so placed that you are getting the shade and shelter and not the people next door. Is it to provide colour, and if so is the colour to come from its flowers, its leaves or its bark? Usually, a flowering tree will only be in full bloom for a week or two at the most, and can look rather dull when it is out of flower, but colourful leaves can make a beautiful display for months, and colourful bark all the year round. Even evergreens offer a wide range of different greens to please the eye, from nearly blue to gold. At the end of this chapter there are some suggestions for suitable trees for the small garden, but conditions of soil and climate vary so much from place to place that you should always check to make sure that the tree you choose will thrive in your district. Keep an eye open for what does best in local gardens, and never be too proud to grow the same sorts yourself. The reason why certain trees are popular is because they are the easiest to grow. One very important consideration in choosing trees for the easy garden is that they should not get in your way when you are gardening. A tree with a short trunk and a bushy top can be a great nuisance, causing you to stoop, or even to crawl, when you want to tidy things up beneath it and snatching at your hair as you get up again. Always choose trees that have a good length of clear trunk before the branches begin. This is particularly important if the tree is set in a lawn. Nothing causes more annoyance and unnecessary work than not being able to make a clean sweep with a mowing machine because you have to keep on stopping to lift branches of trees out of the way. One such tree badly placed can lengthen the time it takes to mow a lawn by three or four times—and shorten your temper by the same amount. Attractive though they are, some weeping trees can be particularly maddening in this respect. Perhaps the most beautiful of all, the Weeping Willow (*Salix alba* 'Tristis', called by some nurserymen *Salix chrysocomis*), with its arching branches and long, pendulous branchlets shining gold in the winter, is the most exasperating, trailing the ground and making mowing under it almost impossible. If you are so attracted by its outstanding beauty that you feel you must plant it in a lawn setting, the most practical thing to do is to have something underneath it that does not need moving at all. One way is to surround its trunk by a brick circle large enough to extend beyond the trailing branchlets. In turn this circle of bricks should be sunk flush with the lawn so that the mower can be run around the edge without hindrance. The result can be very impressive and put most other garden features to shame.

Weeping willow in a brick circle

However, you may not want to go to all that trouble for the sake of getting round a tree's annoying habits, however beautiful it is. In any case it will in the end get too big for the average lawn, and it looks even better in a park, hanging over the water.

There are plenty of other weeping trees that do not cause the same problems, because the branches do not reach to the ground and so do not get in the way of the mower.

One of them is a weeping form of the Goat Willow, or Sallow (*Salix caprea*), which bears beautiful furry catkins, silver on the female plant and glowing yellow on the male. Unlike the Weeping Willow, which can reach 50 feet (15 metres) in height, the Weeping Sallow does not exceed 10 feet (3 metres) and so is at home in even the smallest garden.

Another problem-free weeping tree is the Weeping Pear (*Pyrus Salicifolia* 'Pendula'), which though a true pear with small cream-coloured flowers and insignificant fruit manages to look like a very elegant willow with its long, silvery leaves hanging from its arching, pendulous branches which cascade from a dense head drowning a long straight trunk. It never grows more than about 25 feet (8 metres) tall and is ideal in a lawn or in a border, where its light tracery of branches prevents it from casting too heavy a shadow over the plants beneath.

Among other weeping trees are varieties of Birch (*Betula pendula* 'Tristis' or better still 'Youngii'), Box (*Buxus sempervirens* 'Pendula') and Ash (*Fraxinus excelsior* 'Pendula') which makes a lovely shady arbour with a seat placed within the embrace of its hanging branches. At the other extreme to the weeping trees are those known as upright or fastigiate in growth, which hold their branches stiffly erect and often look as if they had been carefully trimmed although they rarely if ever need clipping at all. They include upright forms of several of the broad-leaved trees such as the Silver Maple (*Acer saccharinum* 'Pyramidale'), the Hawthorn (*Crataegus monogyna* 'Stricta'), perfect for limited spaces, the Laburnum (*Laburnum anagyroides* 'Pyramidalis'), the Cherry (*Prunus serrulata* 'Erecta', otherwise known as 'Amanogawa') and the Rowan or Mountain Ash (*Sorbus aucuparia* 'Fastigiata'). Among conifers there are narrow, column-like forms of Cypress, such as *Chamaecyparis lawsoniana* 'Columnaris', with blue-green foliage, and *Cupressus arizonica* 'Pyramidalis', of which there are blue and golden forms, and the Irish Juniper (*Juniperus communis hibernica*), a pillar-like small tree for rather formal parts of the garden. Be careful not to plant too many of these upright growing conifers, however, or you will finish up with a place that looks more like a churchyard or cemetery than a garden. The secret of choosing trees for the most pleasing effect is to have a mixture of upright and spreading, evergreen and deciduous, and not too many of one sort.

SHRUBS

These too make for trouble-free gardening. If the right kinds are chosen and properly planted, they should more or less look after themselves and only need the briefest attention from time to time. The easiest kinds to manage are those which rarely if ever need pruning, except perhaps for the occasional removal of dead wood or the cutting back of some shoots to encourage new ones to grow from the base.

There are shrubs for every purpose and every taste: evergreen and deciduous, flowering and foliage, shade-lovers and sun-lovers, tall and short. A brief selection of some of the best garden kinds is given with notes at the end of this chapter, but it is impossible to list more than a very few in a book of this kind. There are plenty of catalogues issued by tree and shrub specialists which give pictures and descriptions of the varieties they have for sale. Get hold of a number of them and study the contents, but take some of the more lyrical descriptions with a pinch of salt. Go to nurseries and garden centres where you can see the plants growing. Choose the most popular kinds, the best-sellers; the reason why they are best-sellers is simply that they are best.

Planting and Staking

There are a few basic rules in planting trees and shrubs, to make the operation itself as easy as possible and to ensure that the newly planted subjects are given the best start in life. The first thing is to make sure that all roots of perennial weeds such as thistles and bindweed are removed before you plant anything; otherwise you are going to spend weary hours weeding later on. The soil should be well prepared and fertile, but not heavily manured. Overfeeding is as bad for plants as it is for people, leading to soft growth which is liable to damage by disease and bad weather. If the soil is reasonably good, nothing more is usually needed except perhaps a handful of bonemeal in the planting-hole. The hole should be just deep enough to ensure that the soil-mark at the base of the tree or shrub comes level with the surface of the ground. Lay a stick across the hole and adjust the depth accordingly. Mound up a little soil in the centre and sit the plant firmly on it. Spread out the roots and fill in the soil around them, treading it down as you proceed.

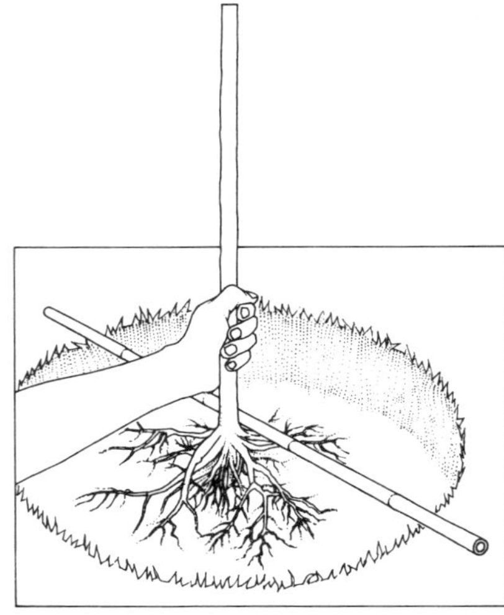

Planting hole with stick laid across to give correct soil level

The ground must be in the right condition at planting-time. This always used to be during the winter, the earlier the better, so that roots would have time to recover from the drastic, surgical operation of transplanting and send out new rootlets before warmer days caused the plants to breathe out more moisture, which the damaged root system found it hard to supply. Nowadays many shrubs, and even young trees, are sold in containers instead of being dug up from the open ground, so the roots remain more or less intact and therefore the time of planting is not so important. What is still important, however, is that the ground should not be either frozen or wet and sticky when transplanting takes place. If the trees or shrubs should arrive when the condition of the soil or the weather is unfavourable, they can usually be stored for a few days in a frost-proof shed without harm. If there is no such shed, or if the adverse conditions look like lasting for some weeks, the best thing to do with the new arrivals is to heel them in until conditions improve. The way to do this is to dig out a rough trench, one spade deep, with one vertical and one sloping side. Unpack the trees or shrubs and lay them in the trench

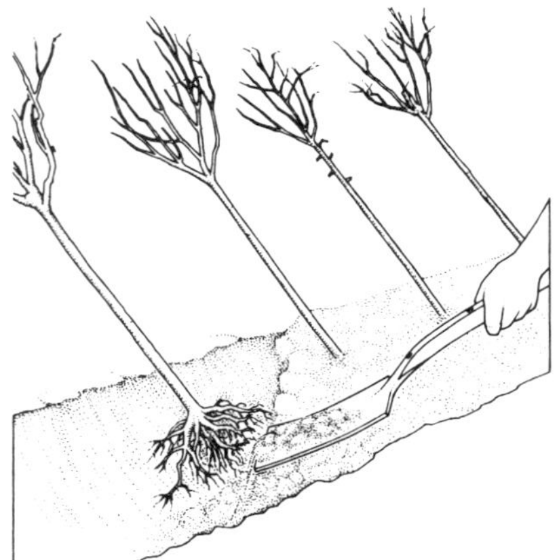

Heeling-in during bad weather

so that they rest along the sloping side. Then heap the soil back so as to cover the roots completely, but be careful not to cover the main stems any higher than the soil-mark, or you will lose your guide to how deeply they should be planted when the time comes. Firm the soil with your heel to keep out frost. Staking is a necessary precaution to stop newly planted trees and the taller shrubs being swayed by the wind, which, besides tearing the roots, can create a funnel-shaped hole in the earth at the base into which frost and rain can penetrate. The stake should be driven in before planting, and the tree secured by a tie. It is important that there should be something between the stem and the stake to prevent the bark from being damaged by chafing. Some methods are shown here, of which the best (and the most expensive) is the adjustable 'belt' which can be loosened as the stem grows thicker.

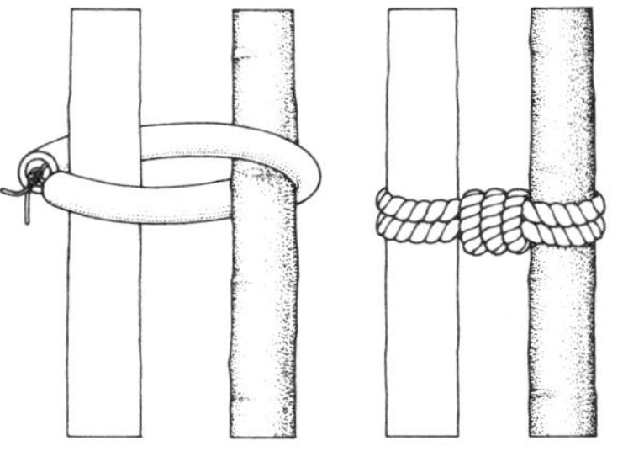

Hose and wire tie *Cord or rope tie*

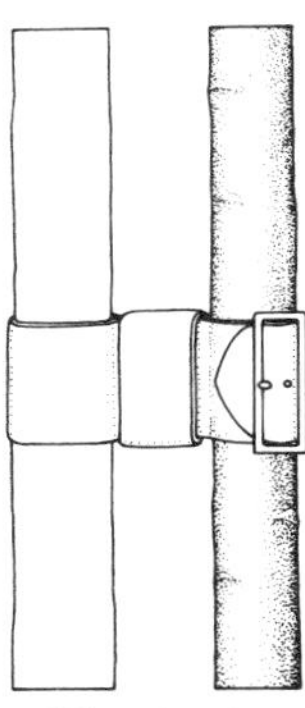

Plastic tie

SOME TREES FOR THE EASY GARDEN

The following will not become too tall and will grow in limy or lime-free soils.

Name	Height ft m	Spread ft m	Description
Acer negundo 'Variegatum'	30 9	30 9	'Variegated Box Elder'. Green and white leaves; silver seed-vessels.
Acer palmatum 'Atropurpureum'	12 3·5	12 3·5	'Red-leaved Japanese Maple'. Deep purplish palmate leaves.
Acer griseum	20 6	10 3	'Paperbark Maple'. Gorgeous autumn leaves. Peeling bark; orange-coloured layer beneath.
Catalpa bignonioides	25 7·5	30 9	'Indian Bean Tree', with fox-glove-like flowers in late summer and large, heart shaped leaves.
Crataegus prunifolia	20 6	15 4·5	'Plum-leaved Hawthorn' with large red fruit and blazing leaves in the autumn.
Laburnum × *watereri* 'Vossii'	18 5·5	12 3·5	The Laburnum with the longest chains of golden flowers in the spring.
Magnolia × *soulangiana*	25 7·5	25 7·5	Perhaps the most popular Magnolia. Will put up with almost any soil and produce every spring its beautiful large white flowers. Slow growing but becomes a sizeable tree in time.

Name	Height ft m	Spread ft m	Description
Malus floribunda	15 4·5	12 3·5	'Japanese Crab', wreathed with pale pink flowers in spring. Many other beautiful crab-apples are available with variously coloured leaves and fruit.
Prunus subhirtella 'Autumnalis'	20 6	15 4·5	'Winter-flowering Cherry', producing dainty white blossoms through the winter. Many other species and varieties of *Prunus* are available, including ornamental Cherries, Almonds, Peaches and Plums.
Sorbus aucuparia 'Fastigiata'	15 4·5	66 1·75	'Miniature Mountain Ash' (often sold as *Sorbus decora*) with extra large clusters of vivid red fruit. Unlike most kinds of mountain ash, this never becomes tall or untidy.
Evergreen			
Arbutus unedo	20 6	10 3	'Strawberry Tree', with dark green foliage, which carries its heather-like flowers and strawberry-like fruit at the same time.
Cryptomeria japonica 'Elegans'	15 4·5	8 2·5	'Japanese Cedar'. The only conifer included here. A self-shaping tree, making a pyramid of feathery foliage which turns deep rosy red in winter.
Ilex aquifolium 'Argentio-marginata'	20 6	10 3	'Silver Holly', pyramidal in shape and never growing too tall.

Malus robusta

SOME SHRUBS FOR THE EASY GARDEN

There are so many hundreds of excellent shrubs to choose from that only a brief selection of some of the best can be given here. All of them will grow on limy or lime-free soil. (Other shrubs which love or hate lime will be found on pages 86 to 89 or 90 to 93, and ground covering shrubs on pages 46 to 51.) ⋆ = Evergreen

Name	Height ft m	Spread ft m	Description
⋆*Berberis × stenophylla*	10 3	12 3·5	A striking sight with masses of orange-yellow flowers in spring against the narrow leaves.

Cryptomeria japonica

Name	Height ft	Height m	Spread ft	Spread m	Description
B. thunbergii	4	1·25	4	1·25	A deciduous species with spectacularly brilliant autumn foliage and scarlet berries.
Buddleia davidii	9	2·75	10	3	There are many named varieties of this beautiful shrub with its sprays of bee-laden flowers in the summer.
**Choisya ternata*	10	3	8	2·5	'Mexican Orange Blossom', with masses of sweetly scented white flowers in late spring and early summer.
**Cotoneaster franchetii*	12	3·5	12	3·5	Among the most graceful of this large genus, with greyish leaves and orange-scarlet berries.
Daphne mezereum	5	1·5	3	1	'Mezereon'. Welcome in late winter, when it opens its scented purple-red flowers.
Deutzia pulchra	10	3	6	1·75	A magnificent shrub with masses of drooping spikes of flowers like lilies-of-the-valley in early summer.
Forsythia × intermedia	10	3	10	3	There are several named varieties of this well-known shrub, which greets spring's arrival with a burst of butter-yellow flowers along the shoots.
Fuchsia magellanica 'Variegata'	5	1·5	3	1	The leaves of this hardy Fuchsia are marked with silver and rose, setting off the purple and red flowers.
Philadelphus hybrids	9	2·75	9	2·75	'Mock Orange'. Many varieties, with very sweetly scented white flowers in summer.
Ribes sanguineum	8	2·5	6	1·75	'Flowering Currant'. Many beautiful varieties to choose from, with long chains of pink or red flowers in spring.
Syringa vulgaris	12	3·5	10	3	'Lilac'. Many varieties, the flowers ranging from deep purplish-red through mauve to white, single or double, scenting the whole garden in spring.
**Viburnum tinus*	12	3·5	12	3·5	'Laurustinus'. This evergreen with shiny leaves produces masses of lovely white flowers from late winter to spring.

Prunus subhirtella

Forsythia × intermedia

Climbers

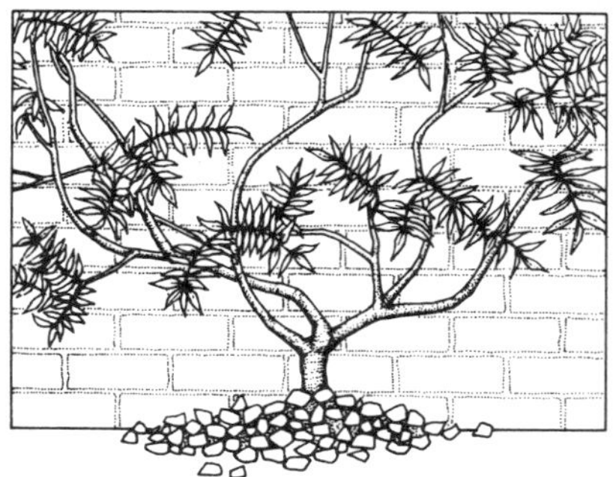

'Mulching' with stones on ground surface to keep roots cool and avoid dryness

ONE OF the best ways to soften the outlines of a new house and to make it look as if it grew instead of being built is to clothe the walls with suitable plants.

The plants too, if they are correctly chosen, will thrive in such positions and get as much as they give from their relationship with the house. Many species that can be grown against a wall are too tender, or too temperamental, to survive in the open garden. This chapter deals with two quite different kinds of such plants. There are the climbers proper, which cannot stand on their own legs and have to cling to something, and the wall-shrubs which, although they could stand unaided, prefer the shelter and/or support of a wall.

Even the true climbers themselves are of two kinds. There are those, like the ivy, that send out aerial roots with which they cling to surfaces, and others, more numerous, that need something round which they can twine their stems, their tendrils or their leaf-stalks.

The first thing to remember is this. *The soil next to a house is nearly always drier than it is in the rest of the garden.* Partly that is because the eaves, and the walls themselves, stop much of the rain from reaching the ground. But a more important reason is that walls suck up moisture like sponges, and the earth itself is warmer near the house and so its moisture evaporates. That is why it is necessary to make sure that plants against walls are never allowed to get dry at the roots. A very simple and practical way to overcome the problem is to mulch the surface of the soil round the plant so as to keep in the moisture, and a very good material to use for the purpose is a layer of stones as shown here. This may not entirely remove the need to water during very dry weather, but it will cut down the number of times you have to do so considerably.

Chaenomeles × superba

The stones will also keep the roots cool, and that is very important for true climbers. The reason is that they have evolved their way of life through living among trees and having to climb towards the sun while leaving their roots in the cool, dark earth below.

CLIMBING PLANTS

Self clingers

Self clingers with their own aerial roots present no problem of support, since they simply fix themselves to the wall. The only problem they do present is that some of them grow so robustly that they invade the gutters and get in through the windows. For that reason ivy is often unsuitable, because it is too vigorous, and virginia creeper must be planted with caution.

Twiners

Twiners have to be given some extra support, since a plain wall offers nothing for them to twine round. Do not put off providing the extra support till the climbers need it or you may find on the day before you intended to do the job that they have flopped to the ground, or even snapped off. The easiest way to provide for the needs of the climbers is to fix a trellis to the wall. You can buy one made of wood or plastic-covered metal from a garden supplier. Do *not* buy one made of plastic alone, since exposure to light makes most plastic go brittle, and a broken trellis would be a disaster.

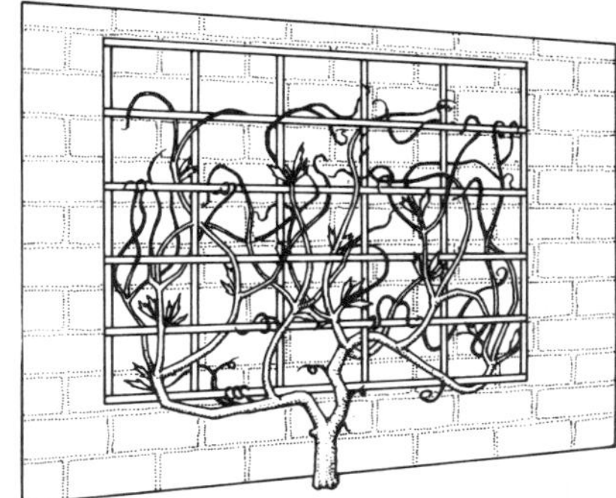

Trellis fixed to wall

An even better method is to cover the wall with wires about 1 inch (2·5 cm) in front of it and spaced about 1 foot (30 cm) apart. These wires should be fixed both vertically and horizontally, so that there is a complete network of supports round which the plants can twine, or behind which their shoots can be pushed if they do not grasp the offer themselves. The best wire for the purpose is plastic-covered multi-strand wire which can be bought quite cheaply. The fixings that hold the wire to the wall are called vine-eyes which are made of galvanized steel and are available in two patterns: the wedge-shaped type which is simply hammered into the wall and the threaded type which is screwed in. Try to stretch the wires as tightly as possible between the vine-eyes for the sake of neatness.

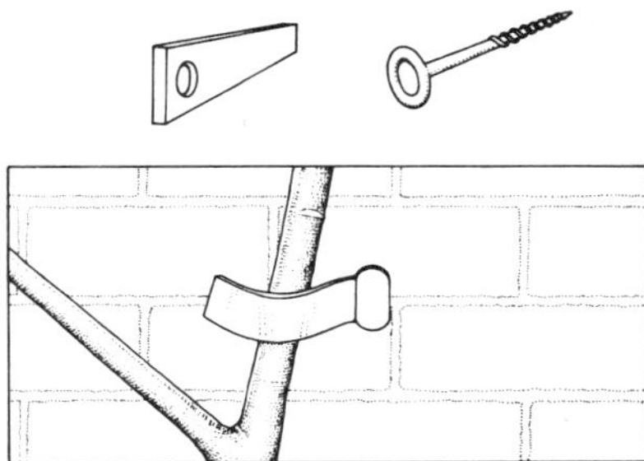

Vine eyes and retaining nails

It is not only climbers that will benefit from the wire support. Wall-shrubs can also be fastened to them temporarily until the branches have hardened into shape. For the odd straggly shoot there are wall nails with a strip of pliable metal fixed to the head. This strip is hitched round the shoot to keep it in place.

WALL SHRUBS

These are not really climbers at all, but since they are used to clothe the walls of buildings they are included in this section. To be suitable for growing with their backs to the wall, shrubs need to be naturally rather restricted and formal in their habit of growth. They must not mind being put in confined spaces and persuaded—or if necessary forced—to adapt themselves to somewhat artificial shapes and often cramped conditions. They must accept hard training without rebelling against it, must not mind being frequently cut down to size and must recover from their wounds quickly. In short they must be domesticated and uncomplaining. However tame it may be, though, there is no shrub so unadventurous that it will not sometimes try to stray from the strait and narrow confines of a wall. Strong shoots will appear which grow with great speed and threaten to spoil the tidy effect. To some extent it is a good idea to let them do so; the purpose of planting wall-shrubs is to soften the appearance of the building, but if you trim back every shoot or leaf that gets slightly out of line you will end up hardening the look of the shrub instead of softening the look of the wall.

Jasminum nudiflorum

When a shoot grows so strongly that something has to be done about it, do not automatically cut it back. *The more upright a shoot is the stronger and quicker it grows.* So first try bending down over-vigorous shoots and fixing them in a horizontal instead of a vertical position. That should quieten down their growth, besides covering the wall better. In addition, if the shrub is a flowering one it is likely to produce far more blossoms on horizontal growths than on vertical ones. Where bending shoots down does not solve the problem and you have to so some pruning, try to do so at a time when it will keep growth in check rather than stimulate it. As a general rule, pruning during the colder months, from autumn to spring, encourages more vigorous growth during the following season, and may result in two of three new shoots for each one cut back. Pruning during the warmer months, on the other hand, tends to reduce new growth. However, where flowering shrubs are concerned allowance must be made for the time when they blossom (see page 114). Wall shrubs are of two types: hardy and half-hardy.

Half-hardy wall-shrubs

These are ones that come from warmer parts of the world and would be unable to survive the average winter out in the open. They are not described as tender, because that is a word usually applied to plants that need to spend all or part of the year indoors.

The description half-hardy means that they can be more or less guaranteed to come through the winter unharmed, or at any rate alive, so long as they have the protection of a wall. The odd one or two may occasionally be killed by exceptionally cold weather, but that is rare. It should be pointed out, however, that newly planted half-hardy shrubs are somewhat tender and may be damaged by frost; so it is a good idea to protect them with straw or sacking in really cold weather during their first winter. After that they will become hardier as they grow older. For some time after wall-shrubs have been planted, the main shoots will need to be tied in place or held with wall-nails, just as if they were climbers (see page 41). Be careful, though, not to leave ties too long. Shoots thicken very quickly as they grow, and ties that are allowed to remain till they cut into the bark can do severe damage. So remove them as soon as the new growth has become hard enough to stay in place without support. There is a tendency for shrubs against walls to grow taller than they would in the open. This means that they may become top-heavy, and the weight of snow—or even of heavy rain—could wrench them forward from the wall. The best way to avoid this danger is to plant them so that the base is at least 10 inches (25 cm) from the wall; then any sudden additional weight will push them towards the wall instead of away from it.

Passiflora caerulea

SOME CLIMBERS FOR THE EASY GARDEN

The following are some of the best and most trouble-free climbers for walls and fences.

SC = Self clinging. Others need support. Aspect = Direction wall should face. ⋆ = Evergreen.

⋆*Akebia quinata*	Purple-chocolate, scented flowers in spring among the handsome leaves. Aspect S or W.
Campsis radicans	'Trumpet Creeper'. Scarlet and orange flowers in late summer. SC. Aspect: S or W.
Celastrus orbiculatus	Bright yellow leaves in autumn. Showy orange and yellow fruit all winter. Aspect: any.
Clematis	A very large choice from among many large-flowered hybrids and smaller-flowered species. Indispensable. Aspect: any.
Eccremocarpus scaber	'Chilean Glory Flower'. Fast growing, half woody and producing clusters of tubular orange or yellow flowers in spring and summer. Aspect: S or W.
⋆*Hedera colchica*	'Persian Ivy'. Large, shining leaves. The variegated form is very striking. SC. Aspect: any.
⋆*Hedera helix*	'Ivy'. Many beautiful varieties, with large, small, green, gold and variegated leaves. SC. Aspect: any.
Hydrangea petiolaris	Large flat heads of white flowers and bold, dark leaves which turn lemon-yellow in autumn. SC. Aspect: N, E or W.
Jasminum nudiflorum	'Winter Jasmine'. The finest winter wall-covering. Its clear yellow flowers brave the harshest weather from autumn to spring every year. Aspect: any.
Lonicera × americana	'Honeysuckle'. This is probably the most magnificent hybrid, with strongly scented, apricot flowers tinged with purple. Many other species and varieties are available. Aspect: E, W, or N.
Parthenocissus tricuspidata 'Veitchii'	'Virginia Creeper'. The finest of all, with leaves turning the most billiant fierry red in autumn. SC. Aspect: any.
Passiflora caerulea	'Passion Flower'. An outstanding climber with spectacular flowers from early summer to autumn. Aspect: S or W.
Wistaria sinensis	Breath-taking with its long festoons of mauve flowers during late spring and early summer. Aspect S or W.

Clematis

Eccremocarpus scaber

SOME WALL-SHRUBS FOR THE EASY GARDEN

Listed below are some of the best wall-shrubs which can be grown in temperate climates.

Aspect = Direction wall should face. * = Evergreen.

**Berberis* × *stenophylla*	Fully hardy, a wonderful sight on a wall with cascades of warm yellow flowers against dark leaves. Aspect: any.
**Ceanothus* × *veitchianus*	'Californian lilac'. The best of all blue-flowered wall-shrubs, covered with blossom in early summer. Aspect: S or W.
Chaenomeles × *superba*	'Japanese Quince'. This includes the best cultivars, with beautiful red flowers in early spring. Aspect: any.
Chimonanthus × *praecox*	'Winter Sweet'. Waxy flowers of delicious fragrance appear in the depth of winter from bare shoots. Aspect: S or W.
**Choisya ternata*	'Mexican Orange Blossom'. A true member of the orange family with scented flowers in spring and polished leaves. Aspect: N, S or W.
**Cotoneaster lacteus*	Gracefully arching, with leathery leaves and orange-scarlet berries. There are many other excellent cotoneasters too. Aspect: any.
Fuchsia hybrids	Many half-hardy cultivars which could not survive in the open are happy against a wall; purple/red flowers, some with white, summer-autumn. Aspect: S, E or W.
**Garrya elliptica*	Long, pale, greyish green catkins in early spring from male plants; the females are drab. Aspect: N, S or W.
Kerria japonica 'Pleniflora'	'Batchelor's Buttons'. Apple-green leaves on arching shoots, with welcome orange-ball flowers in spring. Aspect: any.
Lonicera × *purpusii*	'Winter Honeysuckle'. A vigorous non-climbing hybrid, producing sweetly scented creamy flowers in the depth of winter. Aspect: any.
Viburnum × *juddii*	A beautiful hybrid, neater than its parents, with masses of very fragrant, pink-flushed flowers in spring. Aspect: N, S or W.
Pyracantha coccinea	'Fire thorn'. Ideal for clothing a wall with evergreen foliage. Masses of brilliant red berries through autumn and winter. Aspect: any.
Roses in variety	see pages 72–77
Rubus phoenicolasius	'Japanese Wineberry'. Striking red-felted stems and orange-pink edible berries. Blackberries do well on walls too. Aspect: S or W.

Kerria japonica

Ground cover Plants

Erica carnea

As we have already seen at the beginning of this book (page 3), the list of gardening jobs that take the greatest amount of time and effort is headed by weeding—the hardest, most tiring and most boring job of all. Anything that can be done to cut down the time spent in this unrewarding occupation is a welcome step towards the easy garden.

In a later section, *Defeating weeds* (pages 116–123), ways are shown to cope with weeds when they appear and to make life uncomfortable for them. However, the best way of all is not to give the weeds a chance to make their appearance in the first place. Plants, like animals, have an urge to establish territorial rights and not to allow newcomers to gain a foothold on what they claim as their home ground. The gardener can turn this urge to advantage by covering the ground with densely growing plants which leave no room for weeds to get started. These are known as carpeting, blanketing, ground-covering or weed-suppressing plants, and a selection of suitable ones is given at the end of this section. First let us consider the general questions of (a) how these ground-covering plants do their job of resisting weeds, (b) what sorts of plants are best for the purpose, and (c) how we can give them the right conditions to ensure that they flourish and the weeds do not.

(a) *How do ground-cover plants resist weeds?* They do so partly by blanketing the ground so that many weed seeds instead of dropping to the soil fall on to the leaves of the plants, where they cannot germinate, but remain until they are spotted and eaten by birds and other seed-eating creatures. Of those weed seeds that do reach the earth, many cannot start into growth, because the roots of the ground-covering plants secrete chemical substances into the soil, where they inhibit the germination of seeds; it is as if those chemicals were saying 'This is my ground, and I will not allow other plants to grow in it'. Finally, of the weed seeds that in spite of everything do manage to germinate, most will die in infancy because the roots of the ground-cover plants are so firmly established that they take up the plant-foods from the soil, leaving little or nothing for the new weed-seedlings. That is why in a natural community of plants so few seedlings ever grow to maturity.

(b) *What sorts of ground-cover plants are best?* For several good reasons the best ground-cover plants are shrubs, mainly evergreen, of a dwarf or prostrate kind. First, they cover the ground all the year round with their woody branches and in most cases leathery leaves.

This makes them much better for our purpose than low-growing herbaceous perennials, which, however effective they may be as carpeters during the growing season, die back in the winter and leave the ground bare during the early spring, so that it can easily be invaded by weeds, which being hardy natives germinate and grow much more quickly than garden plants at that time of year. Secondly, even during the coldest days of winter, when herbaceous plants are completely dead above ground and in a state of suspended animation below, shrubs are all the time engaged in living processes, however slowly: breathing, using what sunlight there is as energy for growth, giving out heat, even under the snow, and taking up water and nourishment from the soil. They are always active, and make use of all the natural resources for their own purposes, leaving little or nothing over for competitors in the form of weeds.

Cotoneaster dammeri

Thirdly, these prostrate shrubs are very well adapted to growing in rather poor soil. Nothing happens in nature except for a purpose, and these ground-covering plants developed their habit of growth in order to make the best possible use of rather inhospitable conditions. Shoots that trail over the ground can develop roots anywhere along their length, so that every part of the soil surface is exploited in their search for food and moisture. A well established carpeting plant may have roots in hundreds of different places, and still be sending out new ones as it spreads over the ground. Within a few years after planting, it may be quite impossible to know which were the original roots and which the later ones.

(c) *What conditions are best for ground-covering plants?* Although, as we have seen, such plants are mostly adapted to rather poor ground, it is very important that the soil should be thoroughly well prepared for them.

First it must be properly drained. Though a few carpeting shrubs can put up with, and even enjoy, damp soil, at least for a time, most of them flourish best in dry soil. That is why they grow the way they do, so that their multiple rooting system can seek out what moisture there is. In addition, that mat of closely packed branches acts as a kind of living mulch on the surface of the soil, preventing its moisture from evaporating into the air and being lost.

If your soil is heavy and remains wet for a long time after rain, you will have to improve its drainage to provide the right conditions for ground-covering plants. Single-digging—i.e., to one spade's depth—may be enough to loosen the soil and allow surplus water to drain away if the soil is not too heavy. If that does not do the trick, try double-digging to break up the subsoil, and see if that gets rid of the water. If even that does not succeed in making water disappear, you will have to resort to draining the ground by one of the methods described on page 20. The importance of thorough drainage cannot be emphasised too strongly if you want the soil to be suitable for carpeting plants.

Hypericum calycinum

Next, it is absolutely vital that there should be no perennial weeds in the soil. You want your ground-covering shrubs to take possession of the soil from the moment they are put in, and they will never do that properly if something else is already in possession with a prior claim. So when you are digging the ground to prepare it for their new home, make sure to remove every piece of root you find, particularly of bindweed, dock, thistle and such coarse-growing perennial weeds. And for the first season after putting in the plants keep an eye open for any bits of root you may have overlooked, and pull them out as soon as they start to shoot. In the following years, when the ground-coverers have taken over, there should be very little trouble.

If the ground is badly infested with perennial weeds, the easiest thing may be to treat it with a weed-killer after digging it, as explained in the section *Defeating weeds* (pages 116–123), and then leave it unplanted for a year, pulling up or chopping off any bits of weed that survive the treatment. You will lose a year, but that will soon be made up by the improved growth that comes from weed-free soil. And think of the labour you will have saved yourself.

The traditional planting-time for evergreens, which because they are never completely dormant need conditions that encourage immediate root-growth, is either in mid-autumn, while the ground is still warm, or in mid-spring, when it is beginning to warm up again. Since most of the best ground-covering plants are evergreen, those are the times when they are usually planted. The few deciduous ones worth growing are normally put in during the winter, while they are dormant.

Those are still the best times for plants dug out of the ground, because they suffer extensive root-damage in the process and need some time to recover before the hot weather. In these days of instant gardening, however, modern garden-centres sell a wide selection of excellent plants grown in containers, ready to be taken home and put straight into the ground at any time of the year.

Do not make the mistake of putting a lot of manure or fertiliser into the soil when planting ground-covering shrubs. We do not want soft, flabby growth which leaves bare patches of earth, but hard, compact growth which completely covers the soil. A handful of peat and a sprinkling of bonemeal in the planting holes is all that is necessary.

Prostrate shrubs make an ideal ground-cover in the shrub border, where they form a weed-proof carpet under the taller-growing plants and set them off to much better effect than bare earth ever could. Do not, however, confine them to the companionship of other shrubs.

Use them in the herbaceous border too. Better still, give up the old-fashioned idea of separate herbaceous borders and shrub borders. Join the trend to the mixed border containing shrubs, trees, herbaceous perennials, bulbs or whatever you fancy. It is more natural, it looks better, and it saves a lot of labour.

Genista lydia

SOME GOOD GROUND COVER PLANTS

Most of the following are prostrate shrubs. Some are other types of plants. The important thing is that they all make spreading growth which discourages weeds.

E = Evergreen. D = Deciduous. S = Shrub. P = Perennial.

Name	Type	Height in.	Height cm	Spread in.	Spread cm	Description
Bergenia cordifolia	EP	12	30	15	40	'Megasea'. Thick, leathery leaves and spikes of deep pink flowers in early spring.
B. crassifolia	EP	12	30	18	45	Fleshy leaves and branched spikes of large blood red flowers in spring.
Brunnera macrophylla	DP	15	40	24	60	'Siberian Bugloss'. Large, rough, long-stalked leaves and spray of forget-me-not blue flowers.
Cornus canadensis	P	4	10	24	60	'Creeping Dogwood'. Makes a dense carpet starred in summer with white flowers followed by vivid red berries.

Name	Type	Height in.	Height cm	Spread in.	Spread cm	Description
Cotoneaster dammeri	ES	2	5	72	180	Completely prostrate, with long trailing shoots which mould themselves to the ground. Bright red berries in autumn.
C. horizontalis	DS	24	60	96	240	'Herring-bone Cotoneaster'. Arching and spreading branches. Plenty of red berries in autumn. Fine for banks and walls.
C. microphyllus cochleatus	ES	4	10	84	210	Creeping shrub, making an evergreen carpet of small oval leaves. Ablaze with red berries in autumn.
C. salicifolius	ES	6	15	96	240	'Willow-leaved Cotoneaster'. Likes shade. Splendid ground-cover with clusters of bright red fruit in autumn.
Cytisus procumbens	DS	2	5	72	180	'Creeping Broom'. Forms a dense ground-hugging mat, alive with bright yellow flowers in spring.
Erica carnea	ES	8	20	18	45	'Winter-flowering Heather'. Many different kinds, giving brilliant effect when little else is in flower.
Euonymus fortunei	ES	24	60	72	180	Wide-spreading and self-rooting foliage shrub. The silver-variegated kind is most effective. Good for front of border or under low walls.
Euphorbia robbiae	EP	18	45	36	90	'Carpet Spurge'. A valuable weed-suppresser, but apt to become invasive in borders.
Genista lydia	DS	30	90	84	210	Sickle-shaped green shoots covered in late spring with masses of golden flowers.
G. sylvestris	DS	4	10	30	90	'Dalmatian Broom'. Dense cushion-forming shrub, covered in early summer with yellow flowers.
Geranium endressii	EP	12	30	18	24	A low-growing cranesbill, with sprays of clear pink flowers from early summer to autumn.

Euonymus fortunei

Name	Type	Height in. cm.	Spread in. cm.	Description
Hosta sieboldiana	DP	24 60	60 150	'Plantain Lily'. A strong-growing species with grey-green leaves.
Hypericum calycinum	ES	18 45	24 60	'Rose of Sharon'. First class carpeting shrub for banks and bare places. Attractive leaves and butter-yellow flowers with brushes of stamens.
H. moseranum	DS	18 45	36 90	'St. John's Wort'. This species is wide spreading with low arching branches and large yellow flowers.
Lamium maculatum	P	12 30	18 45	'Spotted Deadnettle'. A more compact variety of the common weed with white-splashed leaves and purple flowers.
Pachysandra terminalis	ES	12 30	24 60	One of the best carpeting shrubs for shady places, with fresh green foliage. A variegated form has silver-edged leaves.
Polygonum affine	P	6 15	24 60	'Himalayan Fleece-Flower'. Bronze leaves and spikes of pink or red flowers.
Potentilla arbuscula 'Beesii'	DS	12 30	30 75	Compact shrub with golden flowers on cushions of silver foliage.
Pulmonaria saccharata	DP	12 30	18 45	A good shade plant with large leaves spotted silver and pink flowers changing to blue.
Thymus nitidus	ES	8 20	12 30	'Shrubby Thyme'. Soft, mauve flowers against grey-ish, fragrant foliage.
Ulex gallii	ES	8 20	36 90	'Dwarf Gorse'. A low spreading shrub, covered in late summer and autumn with egg-yolk yellow flowers.
Vinca major 'Elegantissima'	ES	18 45	indefinite	'Periwinkle'. A strong growing carpet plant with gold edged leaves and rich blue flowers.
V. minor	ES	12 30	indefinite	'Lesser Periwinkle'. Dense carpeting shrub with soft blue flowers.

Vinca minor

The Border

In most gardens the main source of interest throughout the season is the flower border. This usually consists wholly or mainly of herbaceous perennials, which are plants that die down to the ground in the winter and come up again next spring.

Two common mistakes with borders, which cause a great deal of unnecessary work, are to make them too narrow and to crowd too many things into them. Look at the plan of the garden on page 8. Because a straight path has been laid, perhaps by the builder before the house was occupied, directly in line with the back-yard, the width of the border has been fixed by considerations that have nothing to do with the garden. The border is not only boring in its shape but narrower than it need be. Because the owner wants as many different flowers as possible for as long a season as possible, too many plants have been crammed into too small a space. It is not only the look of the garden that suffers. The gardener suffers too, because there is not enough room between plants, and particularly at the back of the border, for easy weeding, trimming and tidying.

Curve to edge of bed in lawn marked out by hose and pegs

Because the plan on page 9 for the same plot has not had that path to contend with, the border has been freed from that rigid formality and its outline softened into pleasing curves. It has therefore been made not only more attractive but easier to manage because there is more room to move as well as more angles from which to view it. It has become a series of pictures instead of a corridor of plants.

A curved edge to a border should never be too complicated, or it will look fussy instead of restful. A good way to make sure that the curve is simple and bold is to snake a length of garden hose between pegs as shown in the drawing and follow its outline as a pattern.

Corrugated metal edging

Where the border is next to a lawn, keeping the edge tidy between them can be quite a chore. Is there anything that can be done to lighten that labour and still keep the edge tidy ? The answer is quite a lot. One of the most practical and ingenious inventions for easy gardening in the past few years is the corrugated metal strip, sold in rolls at garden shops, designed to tackle this very problem.

All you have to do is to sink the strip vertically into the border soil where it meets the lawn, so that the top of the strip comes just below the surface of the grass. This gives a simple guide for the shears when you are trimming the edge. It also gets rid of the need to use the old-fashioned edging-iron for trimming, which meant that every time the iron sliced the turf in order to straighten the edge up the lawn got a little smaller.

In the old days of large estates the herbaceous border was strictly a herbaceous border and nothing else. No other kinds of plants were allowed there. What did it matter that for nearly half the year, during the winter months, there was nothing to be seen but bare earth and a few dead tops of plants? With so much space to spare, the herbaceous border could be sited a long way from the house so that nobody who mattered need see it at all for the whole of the winter. With the small modern garden, every part of which is visible from the house, the trend nowadays is towards the mixed border, containing not only herbaceous perennials but shrubs, maybe a small tree or two, and even a few bedding out plants in the summer, including annuals and dahlias. In that way there is something of interest all the year round, with the changing beauty of flowers, foliage and fruit, and even the sheer eye-appeal of the different shapes of plants.

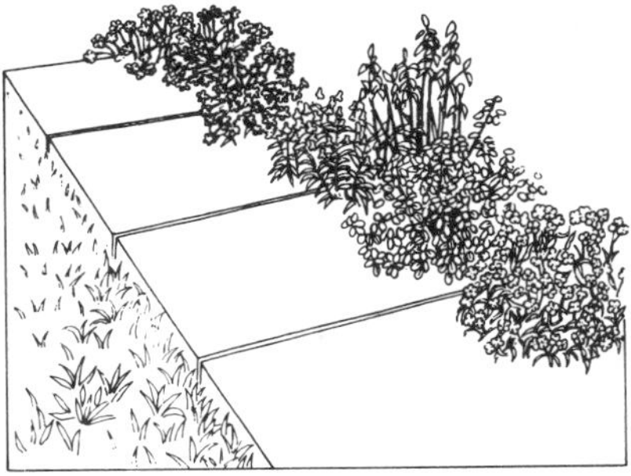

Low-growers spilling on to paving edging whole border

The mixed border is luckily a more trouble-free border. Bare ground is an invitation to weeds, which move in like squatters to unoccupied premises; but with shrubs and trees occupying the border, weeds do not get the same chance of taking over, particularly if there are ground-covering plants such as those described on pages 46–51, which are very effective weed-smotherers. However attractive they may be, low-growing plants spilling over the front of a border on to a lawn make mowing very difficult. The easiest way to avoid the problem is to edge the border with a stone path, laid flush with the lawn. Then the mower can be used without any difficulty and will not damage the plants.

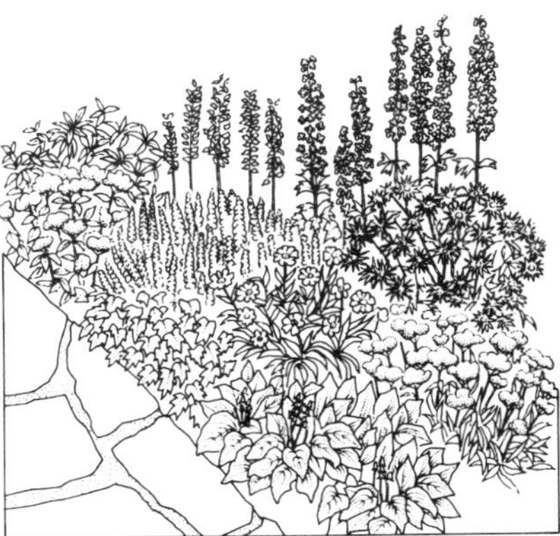

Border planting, large plants to rear, small plants to front

Where there is plenty of space it is often a good plan to have a double-sided border, with tall growing subjects along the middle and dwarf ones along each side. But this needs extra width, which the majority of gardens cannot spare. So most of us have to make do with a border flanked on one side by the boundary fence or hedge. Of these, there is no doubt that a hedge looks better in most circumstances, even if in fact there is usually a fence hidden behind it. However, hedges not only create labour but can create problems too. First, a hedge needs trimming. Even if you take the advice given on pages 30 and 31 to plant slow-growing hedges that need the minimum of clipping, the job still has to be done from time to time. Also many hedges have hungry roots that push their way into the border soil and rob it of nourishment. These roots occasionally need trimming too, to keep them within bounds. Fortunately that is not a difficult or arduous job; all you need to do is to go along the hedge with a good sharp spade and chop off the roots.

Stone or concrete path at back of border for ease of working

But that means that you need space between the hedge and the border if you are to attend to the clipping and chopping in comfort, without trampling on precious plants. Also, since the tall plants are at the back of the border, you will need to walk between them and the boundary, even if it is only a fence and not a hedge, for the purpose of staking and tying. In all too many gardens that means squeezing your way behind the plants and getting your feet dirty by walking on the bare earth. A simple bit of planning can get rid of the problem for ever and make attending to the back of the border no more difficult than tidying the front of it. Simply leave a passage, at least a foot (30 cm) and preferably 18 inches (45 cm) wide, between the border and the boundary and forbid yourself to put any plants there. The best plan of all is to lay a narrow path of stones or concrete along that passage. Then you will be unable to put plants there, you will have a guide line for chopping roots, and you will not get your feet dirty.

The more vigorously your plants grow the healthier they are and the less you have to nurse them. So anything you can do to ensure vigorous growth will save work later, besides making the border look better.

All too many gardeners seem to think that their border plants will continue in their youthful vigour for ever, perhaps because they are called perennial, which to some people seems to suggest immortal. They see the border gradually deteriorate over the years and the plants become feebler, so that they need more staking and tying, in spite of increasing doses of manures and fertilisers to try to restore their lost strength. They also become more prone to attacks by disease and pests and as a result need more spraying and fussing over. More weeding is needed too, as the plants get weaker and less able to stand up to the competition.

Most of that labour could be avoided if gardeners remembered that *herbaceous perennials grow outwards*. The middle part becomes old and feeble after a few seasons and all the vigour goes into the young outer shoots. So each year, when the tops have died down, go round the plants and see which of them need renewing. All you have to do is to cut out the old middle bit—which can end its days on the compost-heap—and replant the vigorous outside pieces, which will do much better separated from the parent clump and living a life of their own. Splitting up the plant like this will of course leave you with several young plants instead of one old one. Resist the temptation to plant them all, or you will overcrowd the border. Just plant the best, and give the rest away to friends.

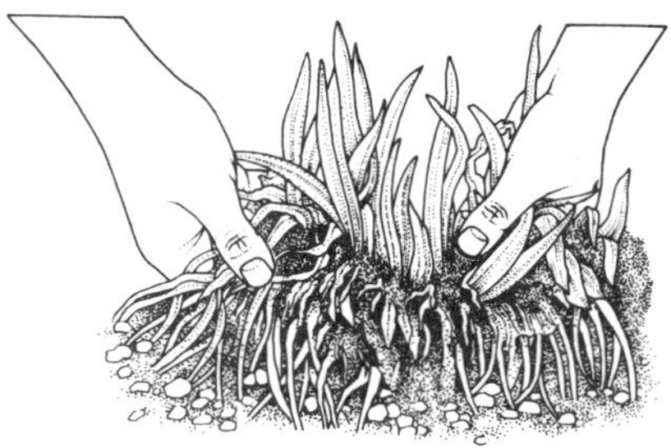

Splitting clumps, discarding centre piece

A very useful labour-saving hint is to choose as many plants as possible that do not need support. There are a great many available, including some that grow quite tall, such as the so-called dwarf Delphiniums, which may reach 4 or 5 feet (1·5 metres), and Lupins, Bearded Irises and Heleniums, which are not much shorter.

For plants that do need support, the important thing is to *put in the supports as early as possible.* The longer the job is put off, the more work will be needed. Once a plant has flopped it will never fully recover, however much attention you give it.

Staking with pea-sticks as plants start to grow in spring

The lower down its stem a plant falls over, the more serious are the consequences; the stem may even snap off entirely at the base. That is why the support should be given early. In fact the rule should be: *always give support before the plant really needs it.* A very easy method is to push twiggy sticks into the soil around the plants as soon as the young shoots begin to appear in the spring. Sticks of the kind used for supporting rows of peas are ideal. The shoots will grow up through them and become self-supporting. Plants of medium height will probably never need any other support; no tying will be necessary; and the result will be much pleasanter to look at than the forest of canes holding up individual plants that are an all too familiar sight in many borders. Some tall-growing plants with heavy spikes of flower, such as *Delphinium* and *Verbascum*, will need individual staking if they are to survive high winds and heavy rain without being knocked over. Wood stakes will do, if you want something absolutely rigid, but usually bamboo canes are less obtrusive and easier to push into the ground; besides, they last longer. Whichever kind you use they must be driven firmly into the ground to a depth of at least 9 inches (about 25 cm); otherwise they may get blown over, and all your staking will have been in vain.

The old-fashioned way of fixing the plant to the stake was to take a length of raffia or soft string, wind it two or three times round the stake, leaving a long end, then take it round the stem of the plant and tie it with a double knot to the first end. It was a time-consuming business and caused aching muscles from having to hold your arms up for so long. Now, for the easy garden, there are much quicker and less tiring methods of tying. The simplest of these, known as the quick-tie, consists of a piece of wire covered with a paper or plastic strip. You simply place it round the stake and the stem of the plant, twist the ends round each other two or three times and the job is done. These quick-ties can be bought in different lengths, or you can buy a roll and cut off pieces with scissors as required. Even quicker devices are obtainable, in the form of wire rings which are slipped round the stem; the ends form a spring-clip which fastens itself to the stake without tying.

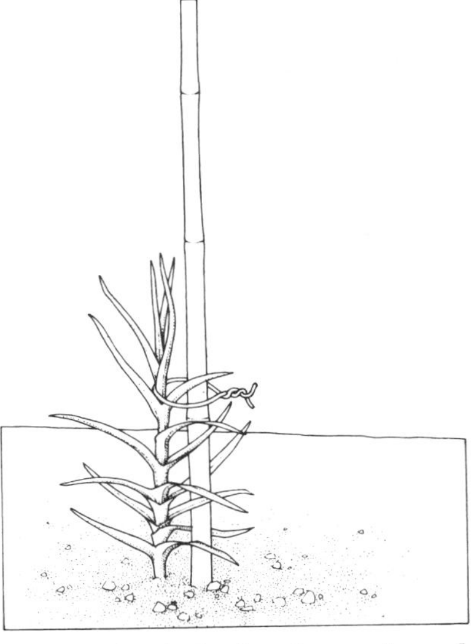

Wire-twist tie for bamboo and wood stakes

SOME GOOD HERBACEOUS PERENNIALS

The following selection contains only hardy, long-lived plants. Use them by themselves or with trees, shrubs, bulbs and annuals. None needs staking, except those marked ⋆ in windy areas.

Name	Height in.	Height cm	Spread in.	Spread cm	Description
Acanthus mollis	48	120	36	90	Magnificent foliage. Spikes of lilac pink flowers in summer.
⋆*Achillea filipendula*	48	120	30	75	Ferny leaves and flat heads of tawny gold flowers in summer.
A. ptarmica	24	60	30	75	'Sneezewort'. Large cluster of shiny white daisy flowers in summer.
Aconitum napellus	48	120	24	60	'Monkshood'. Spikes of hooded blue flowers in summer.
Anaphalis triplinervis	12	30	12	30	'Pearl Everlasting'. Silvery leaves and pearly, everlasting flowers.
Anchusa azurea varieties	48	120	24	60	'Italian Bugloss'. Blue flowers in summer.
Anemone × hybrida varieties	36	90	18	45	'Japanese Anemone'. Autumn flowers: pink, red or white.
Anthemis tinctoria varieties	30	75	18	45	'Ox-eye Chamomile'. Single golden-yellow summer flowers.
Anthericum liliago	18	45	18	45	'St. Bernard's Lily'. Grassy leaves. White lily flowers in summer.
Aquilegia × hybrida varieties	36	90	12	30	'Columbine'. Long-spurred summer flowers, many different colours.
Artemisia lactiflora	48	120	24	60	Feathery silver foliage and plumes of creamy autumn flowers.

Name	**Height** in. cm	**Spread** in. cm	**Description**
Aster amellus varieties	24 60	18 45	'Italian Starwort'. Autumn flowers in pink, mauve, blue.
**A. novae-angliae* varieties	48 120	24 60	'New England Aster'. Rose, purple or white flowers in autumn.
**A. novi-belgii* varieties	36 90	30 70	'Michaelmas Daisy'. Autumn flowers in a wide range of colours.
Astilbe × arendsii	36 90	18 45	Graceful, ferny leaves; plumes of red or white summer flowers.
Bergenia cordifolia	12 30	12 30	'Megasea'. Round, leathery leaves; pink or white spring flowers.
Campanula glomerata	24 60	18 45	'Danesblood'. Clusters of violet, purple or white summer flowers.
C. lactiflora	60 150	24 60	'Milky Bellflower'. Sprays of white or pale-tinted summer flowers.
C. latifolia	60 150	24 60	'Great Bellflower'. Purple, blue or white flowers in summer.
C. persicifolia varieties	36 90	24 60	'Peach-leaved Bellflower'. Papery white or blue flowers in early summer.
**Centaurea macrocephala*	48 120	24 60	'Yellow Hardhead'. Many stems bearing large flower heads in summer.
Chrysanthemum maximum varieties	30 75	18 45	'Shasta Daisy'. Many sorts with large white daisy flowers in summer.
C. rubellum	30 75	24 60	Beautiful autumn flowers in bronze, red yellow or pink.
Convallaria majalis	6 15	indefinite	'Lily of the Valley'. Scented sprays of white flowers in spring.
Delphinium Belladonna hybrids	40 100	24 60	The shorter stemmed perennial Larkspurs; blue flowers in summer.
**D. elatum* hybrids	66 165	36 90	Long spikes of magnificent blue, purple or white summer flowers.
Dianthus plumarius hybrids	10 25	18 45	'Garden Pink'. Many summer flowering, scented varieties for front of border.
Dicentra spectabilis	24 60	18 45	'Bleeding Heart'. Elegant sprays of heart-shaped flowers in spring.
Dictamnus albus	24 60	24 60	'Burning Bush'. Fragrant white flower-spikes in summer.
**Doronicum plantagineum*	24 60	18 45	'Leopard's Bane'. Heart-shaped leaves and large, golden flowers in spring.
**Echinops ritro*	36 90	24 60	'Globe Thistle'. Steel blue, round flower-heads in summer.

A mixed border

Name	Height in. cm	Spread in. cm	Description
**Erigeron speciosus* varieties	24 60	18 45	Many fine garden varieties, with summer flowers in white, rose and violet.
**Gaillardia aristata* varieties	24 60	18 45	'Blanket Flower'. Large yellow and red daisy flowers all summer.
Geranium sanguineum	12 30	24 60	'Bloody Cranesbill'. Intense red flowers opening all summer.
Geum chiloense varieties	24 60	24 60	'Avens'. Flowers all summer. Orange and scarlet.
**Gypsophila paniculata*	36 90	30 75	'Baby's Breath'. Masses of small white flowers in summer.
**Helenium autumnale* varieties	48 120	24 60	Many bronze and yellow varieties flowering through the summer.
**Helianthus decapetalus*	60 150	30 75	'Sunflower'. Tall, with large, yellow flowers, summer and autumn.
Helleborus niger	18 45	24 60	'Christmas Rose'. Beautiful, white flowers in the short winter days.
Hemerocallis fulva varieties	40 100	18 45	'Day lily'. Graceful foliage; summer flowers of yellow and bronze.
Heuchera sanguinea varieties	18 45	18 45	'Coral Bells'. Pink, red or white flowers, summer to autumn.
Incarvillea delavayi	18 45	18 45	'Trumpet Flower'. Rose pink flowers in early summer.
Iris barbata varieties	36 90	18 45	'Bearded Iris'. Summer flowering varieties in many different colours.
I. sibirica varieties	48 120	18 45	'Siberian Iris'. Blue, purple or white flowers in late spring.
**Limonium latifolium*	30 75	18 45	'Sea Lavender'. Graceful, papery flower heads in summer. Ideal for drying.
**Lupinus polyphyllus* hybrids	36 90	18 45	Spikes of handsome, summer flowers; varieties in every colour.
**Lychnis coronaria*	36 90	18 45	'Rose Campion'. Brilliant cerise summer flowers; grey leaves.
**Liatris spicata*	30 75	18 45	'Gay Feather'. Long-lasting, red-purple autumn flowers.
**Monarda didyma*	30 75	24 60	'Bergamot'. Many forms, with aromatic leaves and bright flowers.
Nepeta × faassenii	12 30	18 45	'Catmint'. Lavender blue flowers from early summer to autumn.
**Penstemon barbatus* varieties	36 90	24 60	'Beard Tongue'. Brilliant foxglove-like flowers through the summer.
Phlox paniculata varieties	36 90	24 60	Flowers in wide range of colours all summer into autumn.

Helenium

Solidago

Name	Height in. cm	Spread in. cm	Description
Physostegia virginiana varieties	36 90	18 45	'Obedient Plant'. Vivid flowers—red, purple or white—in autumn.
Polemonium coeruleum	24 60	12 30	'Jacob's Ladder'. Blue or white flowers from spring to late summer.
Primula denticulata varieties	12 30	12 30	Front of border. Spring flowers of lilac, purple, crimson or white.
P. Polyanthus hybrids	12 30	12 30	Spring flowering garden hybrids: gold, red, pink, white and blue.
Pulmonaria saccharata	10 25	12 30	'Bethlehem Sage'. Silver spotted leaves, pink/blue flowers in spring.
Pyrethrum roseum varieties	30 75	18 45	Large daisy flowers, mainly red, in early summer.
Sedum spectabile varieties	18 45	18 45	'Japanese Stonecrop'. Fleshy leaves; pink or red autumn flowers.
Sidalcea malvaeflora varieties	40 100	24 60	'Prairie Mallow'. Summer flowers of pink, crimson, carmine, salmon.
Solidago × hybrida varieties	36 90	30 75	'Golden Rod'. Sprays of autumn flowers. Choose short varieties.
**Thalictrum dipterocarpum*	60 150	24 60	'Meadow Rue'. Fern-like leaves. Lavender flowers in summer.
**Verbascum phoeniceum* hybrids	60 150	30 75	Stately spikes of yellow, pink, mauve or white flowers in summer.
**Veronica spicata* varieties	18 45	12 30	'Spiked Speedwell'. Blue, pink or white flowers in summer.

Phlox

Bulbs and Corms

Muscari

PROBABLY THE most welcome flowers of the whole year are those of the early spring bulbs. They are also some of the easiest things of all to grow. You just put them in the ground, mostly in the autumn, and forget all about them. Then one day, after the calendar has been changed and you feel a year older and it seems as if winter will never end, up they come, open their sparkling flowers, and suddenly spring is here again. For the sake of simplicity, this chapter will use the word bulbs for all the things that ordinary people call bulbs, whether they are true bulbs (enlarged buds), corms (swollen stem bases) or tubers (thickened terminal stem-tissue). The essential thing about them all is that they consist of flower buds with stored food to nourish them, packaged together in such a way as to protect the contents against unfavourable weather, including summer drought and winter cold. Bulbs give us not only some of the first flowers of the year but the last ones too. With the right choice of kinds from the thousands offered for sale by garden suppliers you can have bulbs in flower from January to December. On pages 62 and 63, is a list of suitable sorts, arranged by season; you can also make your choice from the glossy catalogues issued by the big bulb merchants (so long as you do not take too seriously the colours in the pictures or the glowing prose-poetry in the descriptions).

WHERE TO PLANT

There is nowhere in the garden where bulbs are out of place. They give life and colour to borders while the other plants are still deep in their winter sleep; they can be naturalised in grass; they will grow and flower in suitable spaces in paving or rock gardens; they are happy in tubs and window boxes; and since most of them do not mind whether they are in sun or shade they can be planted beneath trees and shrubs. Finally they can be used to brighten up the home itself, either planted in bowls or as cut flowers.

The early spring-flowering bulbs are particularly useful and attractive planted in groups near the house, where they can be seen through the window and will give your spirits a lift while the weather is too cold for you to venture outside.

There was a time when bulbs, especially tulips and daffodils, would be grown in special formal beds, planted in straight lines and standing to attention, like soldiers on parade, with the soil beneath either bare or planted with such things as wallflowers and forget-menots, which were supposed to make a pretty picture by flowering at the same time as the bulbs. Unfortunately, they very often did not. Such formal scenes may look very grand and impressive in public parks or the grounds of stately homes, but they are out of place in the average small garden. Nowadays it is generally agreed that bulbs look much better planted in irregular clumps wherever the fancy takes you. They are also much more labour-saving treated in this way, because instead of having to be lifted and replanted each year they can be left alone to look after themselves for years on end. (The exception to this among hardy bulbs is tulips, which are better lifted annually after flowering, as explained on page 62.) When finally the clumps have become so thick that they need to be split up, you can replant some of them in different places (to give them fresh soil and yourself the pleasure of changing the furniture round) and make a present of the rest to gardening friends.

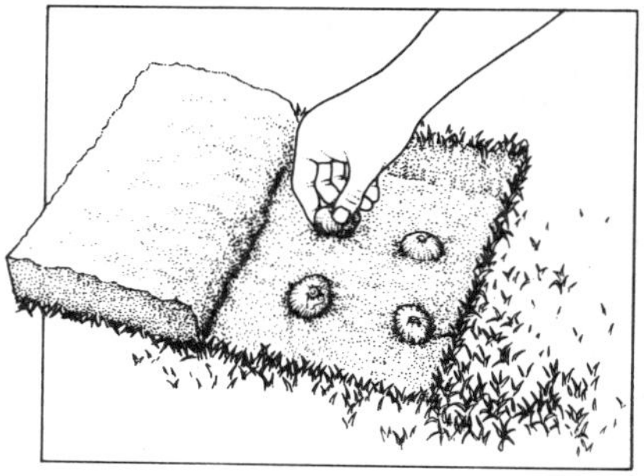

Planting in grass by cutting turf

WHEN TO PLANT

In general, spring-flowering bulbs should be planted in the autumn; the exact date is not important, but if you want to plant special varieties buy them early, or they may be sold out.

Summer flowering bulbs are best planted in mid to late spring, when the soil is warming up and hard frosts are over.

Autumn flowering bulbs may be planted in mid summer; they grow and flower extremely quickly.

HOW TO PLANT

Most bulbs will grow in almost any type of soil, so long as it is reasonably well drained; they do not like to stand in water. The depth to plant them should be about three times the length of the bulb. Do *not* add any fresh manure to the soil. Bulbs are packed with food and need no more. A sprinkling of bone-meal in the planting hole will give them a good start.

Many of the spring-flowering bulbs, such as snowdrops, daffodils and early crocus, give a splendid display if they are naturalised in grass, where they will come up year after year and spangle the green with their bright flowers when there is little other colour about. To plant them, cut the turf to a depth of an inch or two round the area to be planted, slice under it (there are special tools available, but a sharp spade or even a knife are good enough) and roll it back. The bulbs will look quite unnatural if you space them evenly apart, so throw as many of them as you want to plant on to the soil, a handful at a time, and plant them where they fall, so that they give a completely random effect. When you have finished planting them, replace the turf, tread it down firmly and water it if the weather is dry. It will soon knit together and look as if it had never been disturbed. The bulbs will come up through the grass and burst into flower the following spring. It is very important that the leaves should be left till they turn yellow and die down before you mow the grass; it is the goodness in those leaves which builds up the bulbs for the following year. So if you want the perfect excuse to delay mowing till the weather turns warm, plant bulbs in your grass.

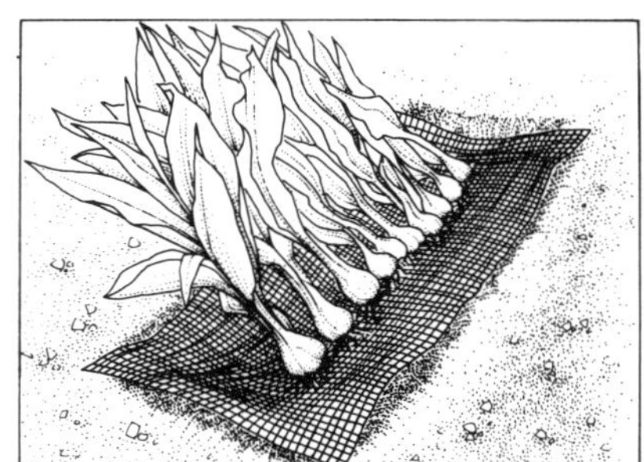
Burying in wire-netting while leaves die down

Tulips, as already mentioned, do best if they are lifted after flowering and replanted in the autumn. Their leaves too must be allowed to die down naturally in order that the nourishment in them can go into the bulbs and build them up to flower again next year. For this reason they will need to be planted out temporarily in an odd corner of the garden until the leaves have become quite dry and papery. To make this temporary planting as easy as possible, lay wire-netting in a shallow trench, place the plants on this, and cover the bulbs with soil. When the tops are dead, the whole wire netting can be pulled up, bringing all the bulbs with it. The leaves can then be removed and the bulbs stored till planting time.

SOME EASY BULBS

For details, get illustrated lists from dealers.
E = Early. M = Mid. L = Late. Sp = Spring. Su = Summer.
A = Autumn. W = Winter.

Name	**Flowering**		**Height**		**Description**
	Time	Colour	in.	cm	
Anemone blanda	ESp	Blue, pink	6	15	'Windflower'. Mass in shade.
Brodiaea laxa	ESu	Violet-blue	30	75	Group in sun.
Chionodoxa luciliae	ESp	Blue/White	6	15	'Glory of the Snow'. Groups anywhere.
Colchicum speciosum	A	Rose, white	12	30	'Autumn Crocus'. Many varieties.
Crocosmia hybrids	Su-A	Orange, yellow	30	75	'Montbretia'. Many varieties and colours.

Name	**Flowering** Time	Colour	**Height** in.	cm	**Description**
Crocus speciosus	A	Blue	4	10	Autumn flowers. Many varieties.
C. tomasinianus	W	Purple, ruby	4	10	Many other winter species.
C. Dutch hybrids	Sp	Yellow, mauve	4	10	Rich colours in great variety.
Endymion hispanicus	Sp	Blue, white	14	35	'Spanish Bluebell'. Never fails.
Eranthis × tubergenii	ESp	Bright yellow	4	10	'Winter Aconite'. The best kind.
Erythronium dens-canis	Sp	Pink etc.	6	15	'Dog's Tooth Violet'. Many forms.
Galanthus nivalis	W	White	6	15	'Snowdrop'. Group under trees.
Gladiolus, tall	Su-A	Various	60	150	Brilliantly coloured hybrids.
G. Primulinus varieties	Su-A	Various	30	75	Smaller; need no staking.
Leucojum aestivum	Sp	White	24	60	'Snowflake'. Graceful flowers.
Muscari species	Sp	Blue	8	20	'Grape Hyacinth'. Many varieties.
Narcissus, garden	Sp	Yellow etc.	18	45	'Daffodil'. Vast choice.
N. cyclamineus	ESp	Yellow	6	15	Earliest and most attractive.
Scilla bifolia	ESp	Turquoise	8	20	'Squill'. Pink and white forms.
S. siberica	Sp	Bright blue	8	20	Fine, hardy varieties.
S. tubergeniana	ESp	Pale blue	4	10	Earliest and loveliest.
Sternbergia lutea	A	Golden	4	10	Satiny crocus-like flowers.
Tulip, garden varieties:					
Triumph	MSp	Red etc.	20	50	Many shades of red and yellow.
Darwin	LSp	Various	24	60	Most popular; vast choice.
Lily-flowered	Sp	Various	24	60	Graceful, waisted flowers.
Parrot	Sp	Various	24	60	Fringed petals; striking effect.
Greigii	MSp	Vivid	12	30	Dazzling flowers; streaked leaves.
Kaufmanniana	ESp	Various	10	25	'Water-lily Tulips' in variety.
Zephyranthes candida	A	White	10	25	Crocus-like flowers, rushy leaves.

Seasonal Furnishings

SO FAR we have dealt with permanent plants, or at least ones that are intended to last for a good many years. There is no doubt that they make for the easiest kind of gardening because once they are in you do not have to bother with sowing them and nursing them through their infancy, but only with feeding them and keeping them reasonably tidy. On the other hand, the quickest and cheapest way to create vivid patches of colour in your garden is to grow plants that only flower for one season and have to be raised from seed each year.

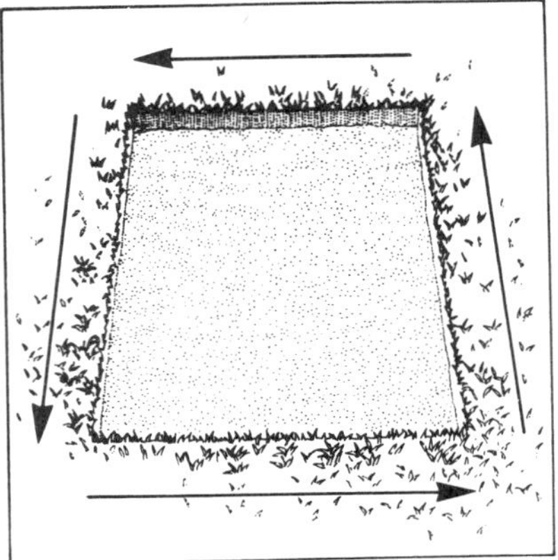

Square bed needs four goes with lawn mower

BORDERS

Seed-raised plants may be grown in patches in the herbaceous or mixed border, where they will brighten up the spaces between the permanent occupants. There is an increasing tendency to use them in this way, particularly where space is limited. They are especially useful in a newly planted border for the first year or two, because they cover the ground between the young plants and look much more colourful and attractive than bare earth or weeds. Some people, however, do not like to use them in this way, either because they object to mixing different kinds of plants together or because they feel that the seed-raised ones will be overshadowed and upstaged by their more established neighbours.

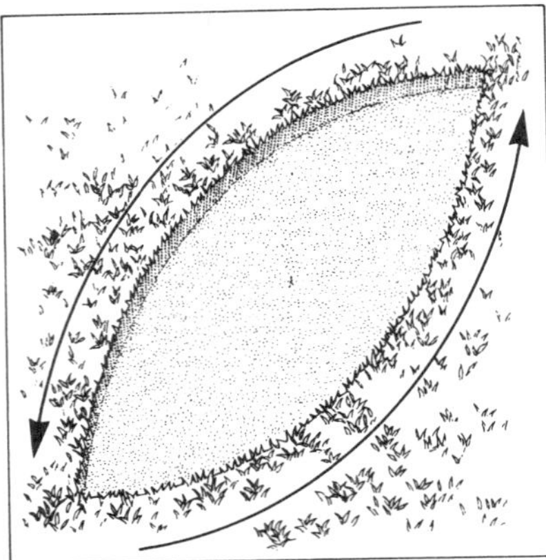

Fish-shaped bed needs only two goes with lawn mower

BEDS

For the reasons just given, or purely out of personal preference, many gardeners still give their flowers raised from seed a special bed of their own. In fact they call them bedding plants, to distinguish them from border plants. Such beds are often made near the house, so that the flowers can be enjoyed whenever you go in or out or look through the windows. Because of the rather more formal house surroundings, the beds tend to be straight-sided, with right-angled corners. That is all right if the bed is in paving, with no edges to be trimmed, but a rectangular bed in a lawn makes quite a lot of work; it takes several goes with the mower to attend to each corner.

A round bed in a lawn takes less work, because you can cut the grass round it with one continuous push of the mower; but be careful it does not go over the edge, or you may damage the plants and skin the grass. Better still is what might be called a fish-shaped bed: that is, one that curves outwards at the sides and tapers in at each end. Such a bed not only looks more attractive and less like the formal ones in a public park or municipal gardens but it shows off the flowers to better effect because you can see them from more angles. It also makes mowing easier. There is less risk of going over the edge and into the bed and less manhandling needed with the mower. The entire grass edge can be cut with two easy strokes with the mower, forward along one side and back again along the other.

Spade tied to string and stake for marking-out bed

To mark out a circular bed, or a fish-shaped one, or any other shape that calls for a regular curve consisting of an arc of a circle, it is not enough to trust your eyes. What may look perfectly regular at close quarters may look cock-eyed when viewed from further away after you have cut the bed out of the lawn, by which time it is too late and all you can do is to chop the edge about to try to even it up, enlarging the bed and diminishing the lawn in the process. To make sure of getting a regular outline to your bed all you need is a peg, wooden or metal, and a piece of string. Drive the peg firmly into the ground at the centre of the circle. Tie one end of the string to it. Measure from the peg along the string till you reach the radius of the circle you wish to mark, and at that point tie it to something sharp enough to slice into the turf. An old knife blade is often used, but a spade is quicker because with that you can mark the edge of the bed and dig it at the same time. Make sure you keep the string taut.

Apart from 'bedding out' plants such as dahlias and pelargoniums (often called geraniums), which are mostly propagated from cuttings of the best varieties—or cultivars as they should be called—the flowers for seasonal furnishing are grown from seed. There are two kinds: annual and biennials.

ANNUALS

These are the plants that grow, flower and die in one season. They are the shortest-lived garden plants of all, but they can give a longer continuous display of bloom than any other flowers. There are two sorts of annuals: hardy and half-hardy.

Hardy annuals

Very cheap and very rewarding. You simply buy a packet of seed, rake the surface of the soil, sprinkle the seed over it and rake it in lightly. Do not bury the seed, or it may not come up; seeds—especially small ones, which most of the seeds of annuals are—need air to enable them to germinate. If the ground is dry, water it. Do not, however, constantly water; plants should have to send roots downwards in search of moisture, but if the ground is always being watered the roots spread sideways and stay near the surface; so if there should be a drought and watering the garden was forbidden the plant would suffer much worse than if it had not been watered too much. Within a few days after sowing, the seedlings will start to appear. All you need to do after that is to remove any weeds (but be sure they *are* weeds and not the plants you sowed) and then to thin the seedlings, which are bound to come up too thickly, however sparingly you sowed them. The distance to leave between plants after thinning varies according to the height of the variety; usually 4 or 5 inches (10–12 cm) is about right for the dwarf kinds, enough to allow each plant to develop properly, but not so much as to leave unsightly gaps of bare earth between them. The tallest kinds will need to be thinned to as much as 18 inches (45 cm) apart or they will become overcrowded. Ones of medium height should be left about 9 inches (25 cm) apart after thinning. It is important that thinning should be done early, otherwise the plants will become drawn and leggy instead of sturdy.

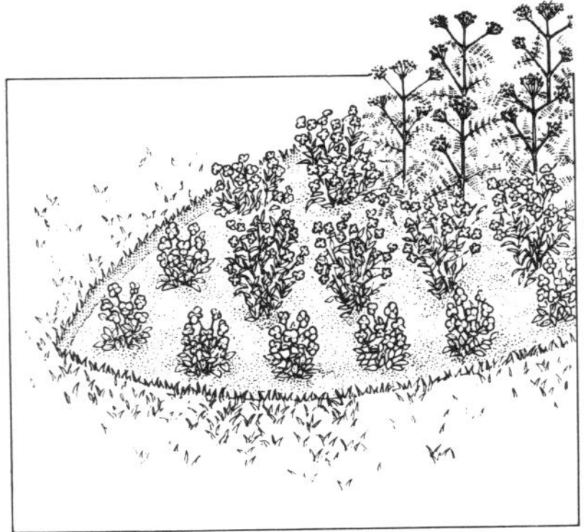

Bedding scheme, tall in middle, dwarf at front

When planning a bed of annuals, give some thought to the question of height. In the selection of species listed at the end of this section will be found a note of how tall each kind is likely to grow—packets of seeds from reputable seedsmen will have the information printed on them. Study those heights before sowing, so that you can arrange for the lowest-growing kinds to come in the front of the beds, the medium ones behind them and the tallest ones at the back if it is a single-sided bed or in the middle if it is a double-sided bed, which is more attractive to the eye.

Most hardy annuals are sown in the spring, so that they can grow steadily without a check as the days get warmer until they produce their flowers in the summer. Some super-hardy kinds which can stand the winter without being killed by frost may be sown in the late summer or early autumn; they will stop growing during the coldest weather but will start again when the days get warmer and so will reach flowering size a few weeks before they would have done if sown in the spring. These autumn-sown ones will not need to be thinned to their final distance apart until the following spring. Since they spend most of the winter in a state of suspended animation, there is not the same risk of their becoming overcrowded and drawn as there would be if they were in vigorous growth, and they do like to huddle together for protection against the winter cold. When spring comes and growth starts again, do not delay thinning; remove the weaker plants and leave the strong ones to flower.

It is particularly important that autumn-sown annuals should not be sown on rich soil, or they will make soft, lush growth which is likely to be damaged by cold weather. So grow them in rather poor soil and they will be hardier.

Godetia

Half-hardy annuals

The term half-hardy is really a cunning way devised by seedsmen to avoid saying 'tender' and so put off potential customers. Half-hardy annuals are ones that come originally from warmer climates, so they cannot stand frost. (Some species that are really perennials in their warm native land but are best treated as annuals in colder places are put into this category.) They will stand the summer out of doors in temperate climates (hence the word 'hardy') but they must not be planted out till danger of frost is past (hence the word 'half'). If they were sown out of doors it would have to be so late that they might not reach flowering size before the winter came and put an end to their life. They therefore have to be sown under glass, in most cases with some artificial heat. Fill a seed-box or pot with seed-compost (obtainable from any good garden supplier), firm the surface, water it, and sow the seeds thinly on it. Sprinkle some more compost or a little sharp sand over the surface in a very thin layer—just enough to cover the seed, but not so much as to bury it. Then place a sheet of glass over the container. Some people cover the glass in turn with a piece of brown paper or newspaper, but that is not usually necessary. In any case, some seeds germinate best with a little light falling on them, and the sprinkling of compost or sand should prevent it from being too bright. Turn the glass over every day to prevent the drops of water that form by condensation from dripping on to the surface of the compost. The ideal thing is for the container to be covered with a domed plastic lid such as that described on page 139; then the water will run down the sides instead of dripping. No further watering should need to be done until the seeds germinate. Seedlings hate to stand in soggy soil; their roots are too tiny to manage to drink it all up and so they drown, or if they survive their growth is delayed.

As the young plants appear, prop open the glass or cover to let in some air. When they are big enough to handle, prick them out into boxes or pots of potting compost; use a sterilised kind, obtainable from garden suppliers, in which weed-seeds have been destroyed and disease germs killed or rendered harmless.

Before you put out the plants into their final positions in late spring or early summer, it is necessary that they should be hardened off. This means putting them into a cold frame, if you have one, or standing them out in the open by day and only bringing them in on really cold nights, so that they get used to colder conditions instead of having a sudden shock by going from warm to cold conditions without warning.

If you have no facilities, or time, or inclination, to raise your own half-hardy annuals from seed, you will find plenty of excellent plants to choose from, all ready to be put in the ground, at your local nursery or garden centre. They save a lot of bother and because they have been grown by professionals with the right equipment they are often better than those raised by the average amateur. Set the plants out in their flowering quarters at the same distance apart, according to height, as suggested on page 66 for hardy annuals.

Nasturtiums

BIENNIALS

These are plants that live for two years, building up their strength during the first year and flowering during the second. They are all hardy—they have to be to survive the winter—and can be sown where they are to flower, like hardy annuals. If you grow several biennials together, arrange it so that half of them flower one year and half the next; then you will not have a lot of flowerless plants at the same time.

SOIL

Unless the soil is very poor, do not manure or otherwise enrich it for annuals and biennials, or they will make too much leaf and not enough flowers. A small sprinkling of fertiliser half-way through the season is enough, to keep up flower production.

REMOVING OLD FLOWER-HEADS

These short-lived plants want to make seed as quickly as possible. If they are allowed to do so, they will stop flowering. To keep the plants in bloom as long as possible, flower-heads must be cut off as soon as they fade, before they have time to set seed.

SOME EASY HARDY ANNUALS

All will grow well from seed sown in the open in spring.
* = may also be sown in autumn for earlier flowering. Height = maximum

Name	Height in.	cm	Flower colour	Description
**Calendula officinalis* varieties	24	60	Yellow, orange	'Pot Marigold'. Very easy. Many glowing colours.
**Centaurea cyanus* varieties	30	75	Blue, various	'Cornflower'. Besides blue, now red, white and pink flowers.
Chrysanthemum carinatum varieties	24	60	Mixed	'Annual Chrysanthemum'. Flowers with bands of contrasting colour.
**Clarkia elegans* varieties	24	60	Various	Pink, purple, red and white flowers.
Convolvulus tricolor varieties	18	45	Various	Dark and light blue, crimson, mixed.
Coreopsis hybrids	24	60	Yellow, crimson	'Tickseed'. Many bright colours.
**Delphinium ajacis* (*Consolida ambigua*)	36	90	Blue, etc.	'Annual Larkspur'. Pastel shades of blue, red, white.
**Eschscholzia californica* varieties	12	30	Various	'Californian Poppy'. Coppery shades mainly.
**Godetia grandiflora* varieties	24	60	Various	Pink, salmon, red and white varieties.
**Iberis umbellata* varieties	18	45	Various	'Candytuft'. Rose, carmine and mixed varieties.
Lathyrus odoratus varieties	Climbing		Various	'Sweet Pea'. Strongly scented, many colours. Fine for cutting.
Lavatera trimestris	36	90	Pink	'Mallow'. Support with pea-sticks. Wide flowers.
Linaria maroccana	18	45	Various	'Toadflax'. Perfect for edging beds or borders.
Linum grandiflorum varieties	18	45	Various	'Flax'. Clear blue, red and white flowers.
**Lobularia maritima* varieties	4	10	White, etc.	'Sweet Alyssum'. Pink, lilac and purple varieties too.

Name	Height in. cm		Flower colour	Description
Nemophila menzesii	Trailing		Blue	'Baby Blue-eyes'. Masses of intense sky-blue flowers.
**Nigella damascena*	18	45	Blue etc.	'Love-in-a-mist'. Feathery leaves; blue, pink and white flowers.
**Papaver rhoeas* varieties	24	60	Various	'Shirley Poppy'. Mixture of many pastel shades.
Scabiosa atropurpurea	24	60	Red, blue	'Sweet Scabious'. Rich colours; fine for cuttings.
Tropaeolum majus varieties	Trailing		Orange, red	'Nasturtium'. Spectacular climber or trailer.

Scabious

SOME EASY HALF-HARDY ANNUALS

The following are sown in heat during spring and planted out when frosts are over. Plants may be bought. Height = maximum.

Name	Height in. cm		Flower colour	Description
Ageratum houstonianum varieties	8	20	Blue etc.	Plushy flowering cushions for front of beds and borders.
Antirrhinum majus hybrids	36	90	Various	'Snapdragon'. All colours; single and double-flowered.
Arctotis × hybrida	18	45	Various	'African Daisy'. Bright flowers of ginger, buff and cream.
Cosmos bipinnatus varieties	36	90	Red, orange, mixed	'Cosmea'.Late-flowering; fine for cutting.
Dahlia, bedding varieties	20	50	Various	Showy annual flowers. (Perennial kinds need lifting and storing in winter.)
Ipomoea purpurea	Climbing		Blue etc.	'Morning Glory'. Large, silky flowers, fading after noon.
Lobelia erinus varieties	6	15	Blue etc.	Very popular edging plant. White and red varieties too.
Matthiola incana varieties	24	60	Various	'Stocks'. Spikes of highly scented flowers, single or double.

Name	Height in.	cm	Flower colour	Description
Nemesia strumosa hybrids	12	30	Various	Compact plant studded with lovely flowers all summer.
Petunia × hybrida varieties	12	30	Various	Many vivid varieties, some with two-colour flowers.
Zinnia elegans varieties	30	75	Various	Velvety flowers in rich shades of colour.

SOME EASY BIENNIALS

Sow in late spring to flower the year after; very hardy.

Name	Height in.	cm	Flower colour	Description
Campanula medium varieties	30	75	Blue, white, mauve	'Canterbury Bell'. Bell-flowers on strong stems in summer.
Cheiranthus species	24	60	Yellow/tawny	'Wallflower'. Warm-toned flowers in spring.
Dianthus barbatus	18	45	Red, white, pink	'Sweet William'. Old garden favourite in many varieties.
Digitalis purpurea	60	150	Spotted throats	'Foxglove'. Modern varieties are much superior to old ones.
Lunaria annua	24	60	Purple	'Honesty'. Dried silvery seed-pods for winter decoration.
Myosotis species	8	20	Blue	'Forget-me-not'. Very easy plant and extremely popular.
Oenothera biennis	30	75	Yellow	'Evening Primrose'. Sweet-scented flowers through the summer.

Roses

Curved, elaborate and labour-making rose-beds

FOR MANY years the rose has been top favourite among gardeners, and it is likely to remain so. As a flower, it has everything: form, colour (every colour you could wish except true blue, but the breeders are working on it) and scent, if you choose the right varieties. The assertion you often hear that modern roses have all lost their scent is nonsense; some of them are more strongly perfumed than any of the old-fashioned kinds.

BORDERS

Many people these days have given up the idea of a separate rose-garden with beds containing nothing but roses, and plant them instead in the mixed border among trees, shrubs, perennials and annuals. The effect can be pleasantly informal, as may be seen from some examples in the section of this book called *Design for ease* (pages 9 and 10). Sometimes, however, the results can be a mess. The trouble is that a great many other garden plants do not go well with roses, especially of the modern highly bred types with mixed ancestry. They have no natural form which can blend harmoniously with other plants; they are really nothing but mass-produced flower-holders. If they are pruned as they should be, they look artificial and out of place among other plants, but if they are not pruned they produce fewer flowers, get out of hand and overcrowd their neighbours, which in windy weather they slash with the sharp thorns on their unpruned branches.

BEDS

From the purely practical standpoint, as well as from the point of view of looks, there is a strong case to be made for giving roses their own beds, with no other plants in them. Roses need their own special treatment if they are to be managed effectively, and you cannot easily attend to their needs if there are other plants in the way. This does not mean going back to the old-fashioned rose garden with elaborately shaped beds, full of curves and twists, like the ones shown here. They not only look fussy but cause a great deal of extra work, especially if the beds are bounded by grass, which has to be kept tidy.

The more curves a bed has the longer the edges become, and the more work has to be done with mower, edging-iron and shears to keep those edges trimmed. So try to make the shape of rose-beds as simple as possible; that will reduce the amount of edging to be dealt with, will make the job easier as well as less tiring, and will look better as well.

A less elaborate form of rose-bed, with a really clean and simple outline, makes maintenance much less effort because it gives you a clear run with the mower and edging-tools instead of forcing you to make a series of twists and turns every time you have to trim the grass. Besides, it looks much more attractive. It shows the roses off to better effect because they have no curly bits to compete with. Grass in the rose garden is meant to be purely a background to the flowers, not to call attention to itself.

Note that roses should always be planted well inside the bed so that they do not overhang the grass, obstructing the mower and tearing the clothes of the person pushing it. This may mean that you cannot cram as many roses into the bed as you could if you planted them right up to the edge, but it will make the job of keeping things tidy much easier.

Well-kept grass does without doubt make an ideal carpet between rose-beds, creating just the right restful background to the flowers so that they look their best. But perfection takes time and effort to maintain, however simple you make the outline of the beds. Many people would settle for something not quite so perfect if it saved all that labour. The most labour saving surface of all between the beds is paving, which never needs mowing, trimming or any other attention. The paving may be of natural or artificial stone and should be of a neutral colour so as not to draw attention to itself but to the roses.

Use of stone between beds eliminates edging maintenance

SOIL

Any reasonably good soil can be made to grow roses. They will not, however, grow well in ground that is badly drained, as is often the case with heavy clay soil. So if the ground in which you want to plant roses shows any signs of remaining wet after rain, the best thing to do is to double-dig it, as described in the section *The Soil* (page 19). In cases of waterlogging it may need draining (page 20). At the other extreme, soil that drains very quickly—usually of a sandy or gravelly nature—should have plenty of organic matter such as manure, compost or peat dug into it to help retain moisture. Since roses prefer a slightly acid soil it will not be necessary to apply lime unless your ground is so sour that a soil-testing kit shows it to have a pH below 6 (see page 17). About two weeks before planting time, sprinkle some rose fertilizer on the soil and fork it in; the rate of application varies according to its composition and will be found printed on the pack.

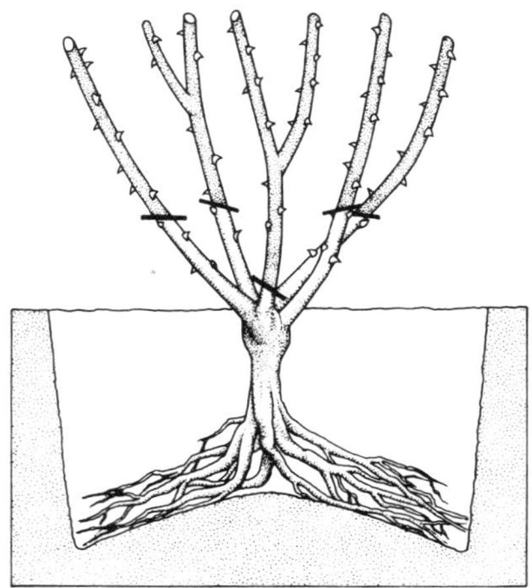

Planting and pruning a rose

PLANTING

All modern roses of the best and most popular kinds are propagated by a process known as budding, in which the named variety is grown on the roots of a suitable kind of wild rose. The point where the named variety joins the rootstock is known as the bud union, and is just above the roots in the case of bushes and at the top of the main stem just below where the branches start in the case of standards. Planting can be done at any time from late autumn to early spring but the sooner the better. The first thing to do is to stand the roots in a bucket of water for a few hours. While they are there the planting holes may be dug. Mound up enough soil in the middle to make sure that when the plant is placed on this mound the top of the roots—with, in the case of bush roses, the bud union—comes an inch or so (2·5 cm) below the ground level. Spread the roots out, place a spadeful of soil over them and shake the plant gently to work the soil round them. Add more soil, tread it down firmly, then more soil, tread it down again and so on till the hole is filled.

SUPPORT

Roses of the bush type should be able to support themselves if they have been planted firmly. Taller ones, particularly standards, which have a bare main stem surmounted by a head of branches arising from the bud union, are very vulnerable to damage by wind. Until they have anchored themselves into the ground with strong new roots, they are easily rocked to and fro, and may be torn up completely by gales. They must therefore be supported by stout stakes, driven firmly into the ground at planting time. Ties must be of such a kind that they hold the stem of the rose-tree, a few inches below the branches, firmly to the stake; but they must not chafe the bark. They should be adjusted from time to time as the stem grows thicker, otherwise they will bite into it and restrict the flow of sap, weakening or even killing the tree. Any of the types of tie shown and described on page 37 may be used for the purpose.

Climbing roses, against walls or other structures, may be fixed in any of the ways described on page 41.

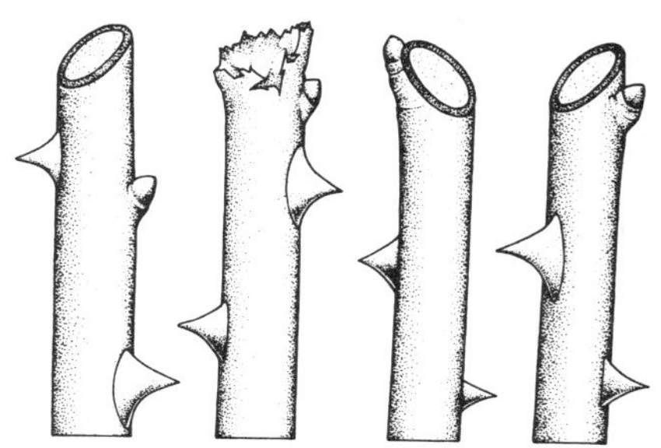
Three wrong ways to prune and finally the correct way

FEEDING

Roses are all too often taken for granted. Their food requirements are neglected and so they become half starved, with the result that the flowers gradually get smaller and fewer, the leaves thinner and the plants feebler. Yet all they need to keep them in vigorous growth are two feeds a year of fertiliser: one in the spring when the buds begin to swell, to help them into growth, and the other in mid summer, to keep up flower production. Use a special rose fertiliser, which will contain exactly the right balance of ingredients. The granulated kind is easiest. You just sprinkle it round the plants and if the weather is dry water it in. Finish with a good mulch of leaf-mould, peat or compost.

Dead-heading floribunda rose

PRUNING

All pruning cuts should be clean and straight; jagged ones invite disease and decay. Each cut should be made just above a bud, so as to avoid stumps of dead wood, and should slope down behind the bud in order to speed up the growth of a protective skin of new bark over it. A continuous process of light pruning is carried on throughout the flowering season by the cutting off of fading flower-heads to encourage new ones to form. Cut just above a leaf; then the bud in the leaf-joint will grow into a new shoot, which with luck will soon produce more flowers.

In nature the stems of roses become feeble and die after a few years of flower-bearing, and are then replaced by young shoots springing up from the base of the plant. Pruning simply speeds the process by removing old wood before it becomes a burden and a nuisance, and encouraging new growth to take its place. This should keep the plant young and vigorous and ensure a good crop of flowers for several years.

At planting-time all roses can be treated alike. That first pruning simply consists of cutting off (a) any broken, damaged or very thin shoots; (b) any flower-buds and fruits, and (c) any inward-growing, twiggy growth at the centre of the plant. After that the different types of rose need different pruning treatment in accordance with their habits and needs.

HYBRID TEA ROSES in bush form are the most popular and commonly planted type. In the first spring after planting they should be pruned very hard, the thickest shoots being shortened back to three or four buds and the thinner ones to only one or two buds. This will cause strong new shoots to grow from the base of the bush and so give it a good start in life. In the spring of the following year, when the buds begin to swell, shorten back the thickest shoots to about half their length and the less thick ones to about a quarter of their length. Cut out any thin or feeble shoots entirely, together with any that have grown inwards towards the centre of the bush. Always aim to keep rose bushes open in the middle, not only because they look better that way but because they are less likely to get disease. Continue the same treatment in subsequent years and ignore the advice of neighbours and friends who tell you to cut the bushes back harder. Unless you want a few huge exhibition blooms (in which case you have to be really savage in your cutting) moderate pruning is best and gives the most flowers over the longest period.

Hybrid tea rose

FLORIBUNDA ROSES in bush form should be pruned hard after planting and moderately in later years, just like the hybrid tea type. There is, however, one difference. Each year cut a few stems down nearly to ground level, and leave some one-year-old shoots from the base of the plant lightly pruned. This will lengthen the flowering period.

STANDARD ROSES, both of the hybrid tea and of the floribunda type, should be pruned in much the same way as the bush form after planting, but not cut back quite so hard. Instead of three or four buds, shorten the thickest shoots to five or six buds, and the thinner ones to three or four buds. In subsequent years be rather lenient in your pruning; otherwise you may, by hard cutting, cause strong new shoots to grow and so ruin the shape of the tree. See that the main branches of the standard are about the same length after they have been pruned.

Floribunda rose

WEEPING STANDARDS should have their branches cut hard back to within five or six buds from the main stem after planting. In later years, the best method is to prune as for ramblers (see below). In the autumn cut out branches that have flowered and leave the strongest of the new shoots to flower next year. In spring the tips of the shoots may be trimmed back.

RAMBLING ROSES are those which grow rather like raspberries, sending up strong new shoots from the base each season. The first pruning after they have been planted consists of cutting the stems down to about 24 inches (60 cm) from the ground. In later years all branches that have flowered are cut right down in the autumn, and the new shoots—which will carry next year's flowers—are tied in their place. If there are not enough full-sized new shoots to enable this to be done, leave some of the best of the old ones and cut back the side-shoots on them to three or four buds.

CLIMBING ROSES should not be pruned at all for the first year after planting; they began as unusually vigorous branches on ordinary bush roses and if treated harshly may go back to their original bush form and refuse to climb again. In subsequent years all the pruning necessary is the removal of dead and worn-out wood and any shrivelled tips of shoots.

SHRUB ROSES are not produced in the same way as the modern kinds and do not need any regular pruning at all. In any case many people enjoy their decorative fruits, which would be lost if the shoots were cut off. Simply cut out dead or overcrowded wood.

MINIATURE ROSES need no pruning, except for the removal of dead, weak or ill-placed shoots.

Rambler rose

Perpetual-flowering climber

Lawns

MORE THAN any other feature, the lawn sets the tone for the whole garden. It also plays a dominant part in determining whether your garden is to be a labour-saving or a labour-creating one.

As we have already seen (page 2), mowing comes third in the list of things that take the most time and effort in the average garden. This section examines ways in which work can be cut to the minimum and still give you a lawn to be proud of.

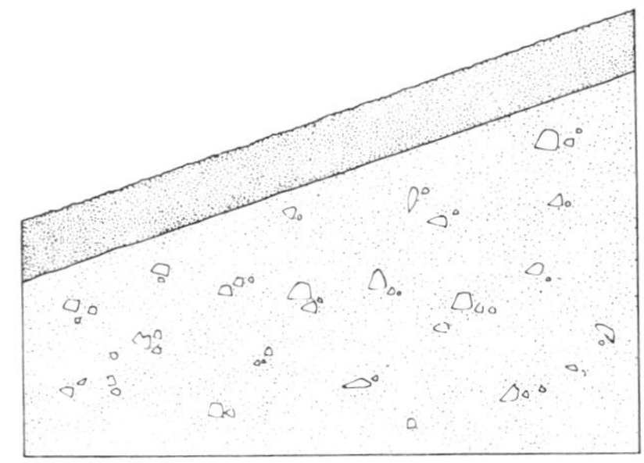

Levelling a sloping site
1. *Remove all top soil*

PURPOSE

The first thing is to make up your mind about the purpose of your lawn. Is it to be looked at or to be used? If it is intended as a show piece with a velvet surface, admired and envied but not to be trodden on by rough feet, it should consist only of fine grasses such as fescue (*Festuca* species) and bent-grass (*Agrostis* species), which look great but will not stand hard wear and are expensive. If it is intended to be played on by children, it should include coarser grasses such as timothy (*Phleum pratense*), dog's tail (*Cynosurus cristatus*), certain meadow grasses (*Poa* species) and rye grass (*Lolium perenne*), which are harder-wearing and cheaper but need more mowing because they grow faster. You must decide which type you want and order seed or turf accordingly.

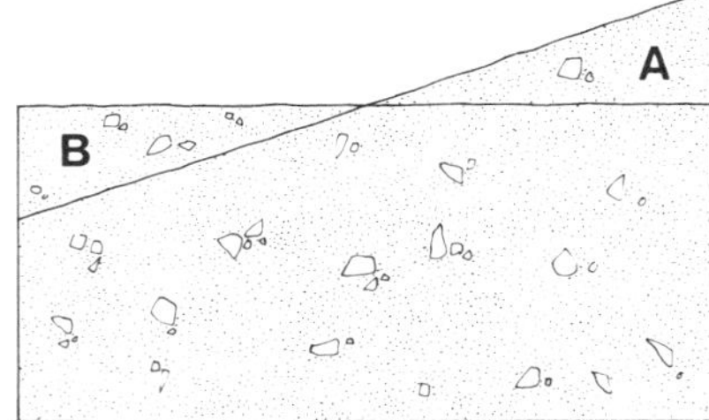

2. *Transfer subsoil from A to B*

LEVELLING

A level lawn is not only pleasanter to look at and play on than an irregular one but much easier to manage. In an existing lawn, high or low spots can be made level by rolling back a flap of turf and taking away or adding to the soil beneath. When making a new lawn, first measure the existing levels by means of pegs, a board, and a spirit level. The height of each peg above the ground will show where to lower the soil and where to build it up in order to make a level surface. The easiest way is to start at the lowest part of the ground. Dig out the topsoil and place it in a heap on one side. Working your way up the slope, remove the topsoil and add that to the heap. Moving the soil downhill like this takes the least effort.

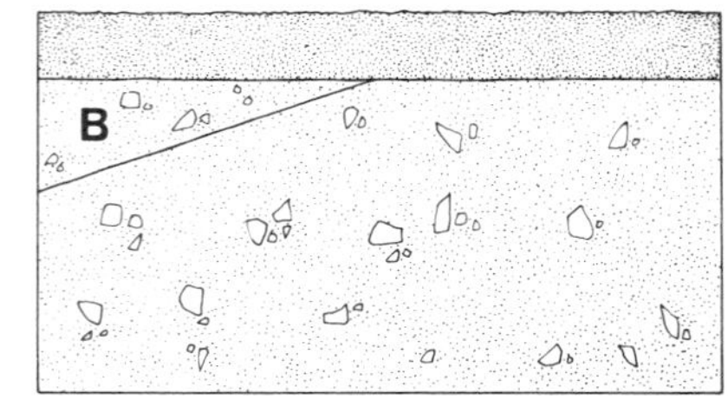

3. *Replace top soil*

Now dig out the subsoil from the highest point and place it on top of the subsoil at the lowest part, which was exposed when you dug out the first lot of topsoil. Continue down the slope in this way, lowering and filling, till the ground is level. Then finish by spreading the topsoil evenly over the surface, tread it down, rake it, make any necessary final adjustments to bumps and hollows, rake again to a fine surface, and the job is done.

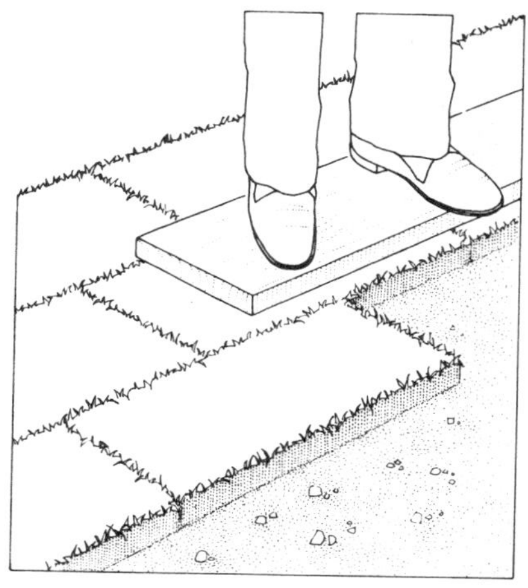
Laying turf

LAYING TURF

The quickest way to make a lawn on the prepared surface is to lay turf. This is obtainable from specialists, or from some general garden suppliers, in oblong strips of uniform size and thickness. These are usually supplied rolled up, to save transport space and to prevent them from drying out. The best way to use them is to start by laying one straight line of them right across the lawn site, placing each one tight against the next to make sure there are no gaps. Next lay a second row close up against the first. Stagger the joints so that they do not coincide with those of the first row. Arrange them instead so that they come next to the middle of the turves already laid. This method of bonding, rather like laying bricks, ensures that the turves knit together as quickly as possible to form a continuous surface. Be very careful that the turves at the edges do not come below the rest of the lawn. If necessary build up the soil under them so that they start a little higher than the rest; there is always a tendency for edges to sink. After completing the laying, sprinkle some good soil into the crevices between the turves and brush this in with a stiff broom. Some people say that you should finish by beating down the completed lawn with the back of a spade, but there seems no point in this unless you want to work off surplus energy. All that is needed is to water the turf if the weather is dry.

Although laying turf is the quickest way to make a new lawn, it is also the most expensive; besides, really good turf is hard to find these days.

SOWING

The cheapest way to make a lawn is to sow seed. Though you have to wait several months before it can be used, a lawn raised from seed is also likely to be best in the end, because the seed mixture you choose—whether for an ornamental or a hard-wearing lawn—will contain only the most desirable grasses. Turf, on the other hand, often contains weeds and coarse grass which will give a great deal of trouble later on. The best time to sow the seed is in the late summer or early autumn; then it will have grown enough to establish itself, but not so much as to need mowing before the winter. This is important, because young grass seedlings are very easily torn up by the mower. It is possible to get satisfactory results by sowing in the spring, but the danger is that a dry spell may occur, and unless you keep watering the young seedlings will shrivel and die.

The other advantage of autumn sowing is that you can prepare the ground in the spring and leave it bare throughout the summer, chopping off weeds with a hoe as they appear so that there are no weed-seeds left by sowing-time. Tell your seed-merchant how big an area you want to sow, and he will tell you how much seed you need. If the seed is bought in packets, the printed instructions will give the rate at which to sow. To make sure of sowing evenly, divide the ground into a number of equal strips by means of strings stretched between pegs. Divide the seed into the same number of portions as there are strips and sow each strip with one of those portions. After sowing, rake the seed in lightly. If seed-eating birds are troublesome, you can keep them at bay by stretching black thread, tied to a stick at each end, across the surface. This will snatch at their feet and discourage them. Do not mow a newly sown lawn until the grass is well established. Preferably wait till the following spring. For the first mowing, set the blades of the mower as high as they will go, so that the young grass seedlings are lightly topped rather than shorn. They need a fair amount of leaf in order to make their roots.

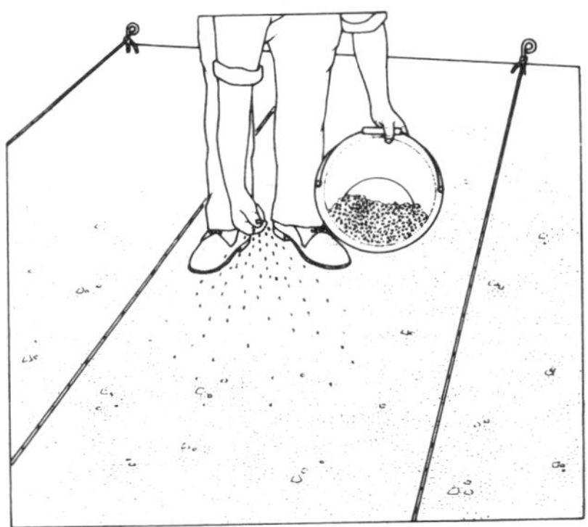

Dividing a plot with strings and sowing in strips

WEEDS

However pure the seed-mixture was, however thoroughly the ground was prepared and however many times you hoed it, sooner or later weeds are bound to make their appearance. You can then do one of two things. You can take the easy line and say that a few weeds do not matter, that a patch purely of grass with nothing else growing in it is quite unnatural (which is true), that really coarse weeds will be destroyed by mowing (which is also true) and that the rest will die out after a time (which is quite untrue). Or you can take the opposite line and set about trying to exterminate every single weed, counting it as a black mark against yourself if any survives. If you show real dedication you may succeed, but only for a time, because weed seeds will always be blowing in from neighbouring ground. The best attitude for the easy-going gardener is somewhere between these two extremes. He will destroy the worst weeds by regular mowing, control the controllable ones with weedkiller, and not bother about the rest (which, being unobtrusive enough to escape the attention of mower and weedkiller, will escape the attention of friends and relations too). Lawn-sand—an old fashioned weedkiller which burns up broad-leaved weeds—is mildly effective, but best are the modern selective weedkillers based on hormones. They may be bought in liquid form, to be mixed with water and sprayed on the grass or applied with a watering-can. Better still is the dry, granular form which can be easily applied by means of a dispenser, consisting of a hopper on wheels which is pushed to and fro across the lawn, a strip at a time. This granular form contains grass fertilizer, so it feeds as it weeds.

Wheeled fertiliser or weedkiller dispenser

MOWING

The reason why mowing is necessary is not just to keep the grass short and nice to look at but to make it grow more densely together so that there are no thin or bare places. If the grass is prevented from growing tall, it will branch out sideways instead.

The greatest labour-saving rule, which cuts down effort and makes mowing almost a pleasure, is this: *mow little and often.* During the summer, when the grass is growing strongly, this means on average, allowing for different weather conditions, that it should be mown twice a week. In spring and autumn the frequency may be reduced to once a week, and in the winter no mowing will be needed unless very mild weather causes sudden growth, when a light 'topping' may be given. At no time should the blades of the mower be set at their lowest, or the lawn will be scalped instead of mown. The best height of cut is between 1 inch (2·5 cm) and ¾ inch (2 cm) during the summer and should be raised during the rest of the year to about 1¼ inches (3 cm).

In this way, by cutting moderately and often, there is very little new growth to be removed at each mowing, so hardly any effort is needed. You can walk forward at a steady pace, without having to slow down and push hard in order to tackle overgrown clumps, or worse still having to use a series of backward and forward stabs, which are not only tiring but do a lot of damage to the grass and may even tear it up by the roots.

If you want to achieve a neat effect of regular, parallel dark and light stripes (the contrast being caused by the light striking on grass which has been cut in opposite directions), you can easily do so by following the route shown in the illustration. It is very important that each mowing should be done at right angles to the last. That is if one mowing is carried out so that the stripes run east to west, the next one should be done so that they run north to south. In this way you will make sure that the surface of the lawn does not become corrugated over a period to time by continual mowing in one direction only.

There are basically two kinds of mower: the cylinder type and the rotary type. Cylinder models, which are the more usual, are the ones in which the blades roll forward as the machine is pushed along; of these, the kinds with side wheels are cheaper, but the kinds with rollers are easier to use because you can run them right along the edge of the lawn without damaging it.

Rotary mowers have blades that spin round horizontally in a wide circle just above the surface of the ground. They are very useful for somewhat rougher grass, but they do not give such a smooth finish as cylinder types do.

In addition to the models pushed by hand, cylinder mowers are obtainable with motors, driven by petrol or electricity. All rotary mowers have the blades driven by a motor, including the latest type which is based on the hovercraft principle and rides on a cushion of air, so that it is very light to handle. There is no doubt that a motor mower takes much of the effort out of mowing, but before buying one ask yourself if the size of your lawn justifies the extra cost. Unless your lawn measures at least 150 square yards (140 square metres) it is very doubtful whether a motor mower is worthwhile.

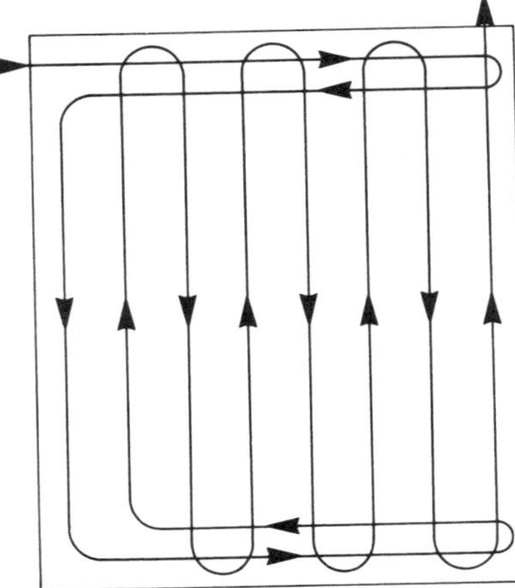

How to get parallel stripes when mowing

EDGING

For easy gardening, have as few edges to your lawn as possible. In particular, avoid having a lot of flower-beds cut out of the lawn; they will take a great deal of time and work to keep the edges tidy. Where you have a path beside a lawn, it is possible to avoid having to do any edging at all, if you make the level of the path come just below that of the grass surface.

Where you do have an edge that needs trimming to make it tidy, do the job after the first mowing of the spring. You can use a spade, but a half-moon edging iron is better. To make sure of a straight edge, lay a wooden board along it and use this to guide the blade. To make sure that the edge cannot collapse, slope the cut slightly outwards. Do not use the edging-iron for the rest of the season, or you will reduce the size of your lawn. Use long-handled edging shears after every mowing, to trim off overhanging grass.

Using a half-moon edging-iron with board

FEEDING

Unfortunately there is no other part of the garden that is taken so much for granted as the lawn. People who would never neglect to feed the rest of the garden ignore the needs of grass and allow it to starve. Yet in fact the lawn needs more food, not less, than any other part (except perhaps for the vegetable garden).

The reason why feeding the lawn is so necessary is that every grass-box full of mowings cut and removed during the season takes away nourishment. In the course of the year the amount of grass removed from the average garden in this way is far greater than that of flower-heads cut off or branches pruned. If that goodness is not put back into the soil, the good grass is bound to deteriorate and the coarser wild grasses will take over, together with other weeds because they are much better able to withstand starvation.

Using edging-shears

You may wonder why the answer is not simply to let the mowings lie on the ground and so return their goodness to the soil. The reason is that decaying grass-clippings (a) look unsightly, (b) can stifle the finer grasses and (c) encourage worms which can be a great nuisance. So always use the mower with its grass-box, and put the clippings on the compost-heap. You can mix up your own lawn-fertilizer, but it is a boring and time-wasting job, and the result is no better—and probably little, if any, cheaper—than a ready-made product bought from a garden supplier. The easiest to use is that sold in granular form and there are two grades; one for the spring, to encourage vigorous leaf-growth, and one for autumn, to build strong roots. Just those two applications are all that is needed each year, and the easiest way to apply the material is with a wheeled dispenser shown on page 81.

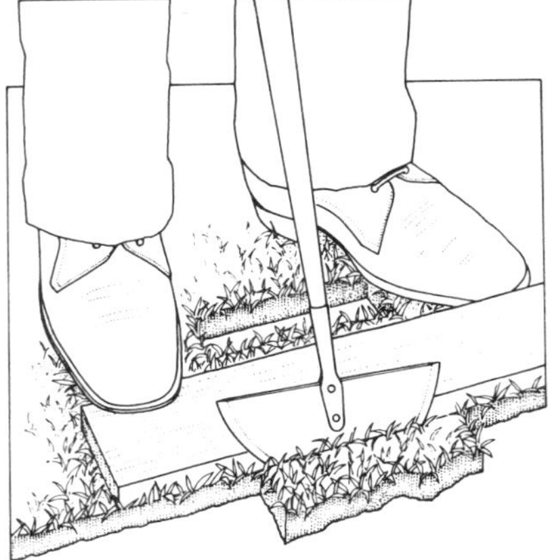

Repairing broken edges

REPAIRING

The edge of a lawn can only too easily be damaged by a careless step, or simply by wear and tear. Not only are such damaged edges unsightly but they make mowing more difficult and they invite weeds. The easiest way to repair the edge is to cut out a square of turf containing the broken part, using a sharp spade or edging iron. Move the square of turf forward on to the path or bed until the broken bit is outside the lawn. Then lay a board across the turf, line it up with the edge on each side, and use it as a guide to trim off the damaged piece. This will leave a gap behind the square of turf that was moved forward. This gap can be filled either with a piece of turf taken from a place where it will not be missed or with soil, firmed, raked and sown with suitable grass-seed.

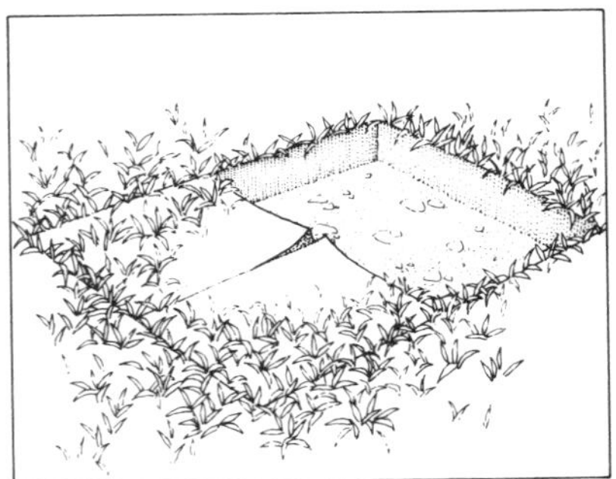

Returfing a bare patch

Sometimes you get a bare patch in the lawn caused by wear, by scalping with the mower, by the removal of weeds or by the unwanted attention of dogs or cats. If the trouble is not bad and the area not large you can rake the surface, sprinkle grass-seed and hope for the best. A more thorough method is likely to give better results. Remove a square of turf sufficiently large to contain the bare patch with a little to spare all round it, loosen the soil with a fork and cover it either with new turf or with fresh soil raked fine, sown with grass-seed, trodden firmly, and then raked again. If necessary, protect the newly sown patch against birds by means of black thread.

The best time to carry out repairs is the autumn. Next best is the spring. If repairs are done in the summer, the newly turfed or newly sown patches may suffer from drought and you will have to water them (if you are allowed to do so, but during a drought there may be a law against it).

SPIKING

By the autumn, the surface will have become packed hard through use and constant mowing. It can then be very much improved by spiking to let in some air. Special spikers are on sale, but for a small area an ordinary garden fork pushed into the surface at intervals of 9 inches (20 cm) is perfectly satisfactory.

Spiking lawn with fork

RAKING

Before the winter, go over the surface with a flexible wire rake to break up matted clumps and remove tangled patches of moss.

TOP-DRESSING

In addition to removing plant food, constant mowing removes organic matter. So in addition to feeding with fertilizer, the lawn benefits greatly from being top-dressed in autumn, after spiking and raking, with peat—or, in heavy soils, with a mixture of peat and sand.

Lime-Lovers

SO FAR the plants listed in this book for different purposes have one thing in common. They have all been chosen for their indifference to the question of whether there is lime in the soil or not. They can put up with the presence of lime or the absence of it. In short they can take it or leave it alone.

Paeony

A great many people whose only wish is to have as easy a garden as possible will be quite content to leave the matter there. They will choose from those lists, and from seedsmen and plant suppliers, only those plants to which the presence or absence of lime is not a matter of life and death. In that way they will be happy in the knowledge that so long as the other growing conditions are right there is no need to bother with the subject; the undemanding plants they choose will thrive whether or not the soil round their roots contains lime (usually in the form of chalk). Some plants, however, are exceptionally choosy. They are the lime-lovers and the lime-haters, and they will simply refuse to grow properly if in the one case there is no lime in the soil and in the other case there is. Each of these two sections contains plants of outstanding beauty and character. That is why this section and the next are devoted to their needs and preferences.

First, it is fair to say that the lovers—in this as in other spheres of life—are more tolerant than the haters. In other words, while a great many of the plants that prefer to grow in limy soil manage to do very well without it (or with very little of it), the really bigoted lime-haters will have nothing to do with it at all; the slightest trace of lime in the soil will cause the leaves to turn yellow and fall off and the plant will rapidly die—or linger on in such a sickly condition that it is kindest to end its misery by pulling it up and putting it on the bonfire. In extreme cases of lime intolerance, the plant will refuse to put out any roots at all, rather than have them touch lime or chalk.

Some gardeners who welcome a challenge, and can find nothing better to do with their time than waste it on unnecessary work, attempt to outwit nature by changing the soil and applying expensive chemicals so that they can grow the lime-haters (or lime-lovers) which their neighbours—less energetic, or poorer, or simply more sensible—cannot grow and probably do not want to anyway. This book is not for such over-active people, because what they believe in is not easy gardening but hard gardening. *Easy gardening tries wherever possible to cooperate with nature, not to fight it.*

To start with the lime-lovers, let us consider what plants are particularly suited to gardens with chalky soil. This can be recognised by the white particles in it and by its high pH, indicating an alkaline condition, as shown by a soil-testing kit designed to measure the degree of acidity (see page 17).

Gardeners with soil of this kind, so long as they do not try to grow the impossible, have a very wide choice of excellent plants which are happy in chalky ground, always provided that it has sufficient depth of topsoil. Solid chalk with only a very thin layer of soil on the surface will grow very little until it has been broken up and had plenty of manure, compost, peat or other organic material mixed in with it.

Syringa

SHRUBS AND TREES

A selection particularly suited to limy soils follows on pages 88 and 89. If any special favourite of yours does not appear there, it will still probably be all right, *so long as it does not appear in the list of lime-haters on pages 91 to 93.* To make quite sure, check with a local nursery or garden centre, which has to stock the things that do best in the soil prevalent in your district.

HERBACEOUS PERENNIALS

Nearly all of these do well in limy soil, particularly the strong-growing kinds with thick, vigorous roots. Almost the only well-known perennial that is not very happy in the presence of lime is the Lupin, though peat round the roots may help.

BULBS AND CORMS

All of the popular ones revel in limy soil, with the exception of some lime-hating lilies.

SOME EASY LIME-LOVERS

All the following trees and shrubs are happy with chalk in the soil though most could manage without it.
★ = Evergreen. E = Early. M = Mid. L = Late. Sp = Spring. Su = Summer. A = Autumn. W = Winter. Height = maximum.

Name	Flowering Time	Colour	Height in.	cm	Description
Abelia × grandiflora	Su-A	Pink/Purple	96	240	Excellent late flowering shrub. Funnel-shaped, flesh-pink flowers.
★*Arbutus unedo*	A	Pink	240	600	'Strawberry Tree'. Fruits hang at the same time as the flowers.
Buddleia alternifolia	ESu	Lilac	180	450	Beautiful pendant small tree, wreathed in fragrant flowers.
Caryopteris × clandonensis	A	Blue	36	90	'Blue Spiraea'. Late flowering, laden with eager bees.
Ceratostigma willmottianum	Su-A	Bright	36	90	'Shrubby Plumbago'. Flowers followed by russet seed-heads.
★*Cistus × cyprius*	LSp	White	96	240	'Rock Rose'. Lovely species; petals with deep crimson blotch.
Cotinus coggygria	Su	Purple	180	450	'Smoke Bush'. Varieties also with plum-coloured leaves.
★*Daphne cneorum*	Sp	Rose	12	30	'Garland Flower'. Very sweet-scented blossoms.
★*Erica carnea* varieties	W-Sp	Various	12	30	'Winter Heath'. First class varieties in many colours.
★*E. mediterranea*	ESp	Rosy red	48	120	Vigorous grower. Purple and pure white kinds too.
Euonymus elatus	Sp	Green	96	240	Feathery green leaves in spring, turning pink in autumn.
E. europaeus varieties	Sp	Green	120	300	Beautiful berries, rosy red splitting to show orange seeds.
★*Escallonia* hybrids	Su	Rose etc.	96	240	Many brilliant varieties in different colours, including white

Spiraea

Name	Flowering Time	Colour	Height in.	cm	Description
Fuchsia magellanica 'Riccartonii'	Su-A	Red/Purple	72	180	The hardiest fuchsia. Many other beautiful varieties.
Paeonia delavayi	ESu	Deepest crimson	60	150	Most striking dark red flowers with bright yellow stamens.
P. × *lemoinei* varieties	ESu	Gold etc.	60	150	Hybrid yellow tree-paeonies in a gorgeous variety of colours.
P. suffruticosa varieties	ESu	Various	60	150	'Tree Paeony'. Superb varieties in purple, carmine, pink and white.
Rhus typhina	Su	Velvety	120	300	'Stag's Horn Sumach'. Ferny leaves, orange-red in autumn.
**Rosmarinus officinalis*	Sp	Blue	84	210	'Rosemary'. Well loved aromatic shrub, with intense blue flowers.
**Ruscus aculeatus*	Sp	Green, small	30	75	'Butcher's Broom'. Self-fertile varieties give large red berries.
**Santolina chamaecyparissus*	Su	Yellow	24	60	'Cotton Lavender'. More compact if grown in poor soil.
Spiraea × *arguta*	Sp	White	84	210	'Bridal Wreath'. Festooned in spring with charming flowers.
S. japonica varieties	Su	Various	60	150	Carmine, rose-pink and deep red flowers in plate-like heads.
Symphoricarpos albus laevigatus	Su	Pink	96	240	'Snowberry'. The best white-berried variety of all.
Viburnum opulus	LSp	White	180	450	'Guelder-rose'. Scented flowers; flat clusters of red berries.
V. carlesii	Sp	Warm White	72	180	Delicious clove-scented flowers. Does well in light shade.
Weigela florida 'Variegata'	ESu	Pink	96	240	Leaves margined with white. Flowers coloured strawberry-ice.
W. hybrids	ESu	Various	96	240	Funnel-shaped flowers in shades of crimson, rose and pink.

Cistus

Lime-Haters

Camellia japonica

Rhododendron hybrid

As already explained in the section headed *The soil* and emphasised again in *Lime-lovers*, if your soil is limy it is a waste of time and effort to attempt to grow certain plants—such as most of the heathers and all of the rhododendrons—which cannot stand lime. True, some modern chemicals known as sequestrols have been developed which can overcome the problem for a time, but they are expensive, their effects do not last long, so the dose has to be repeated, and the results are often far from satisfactory. Within the past few years it has been discovered that the real problem with these plants is not so much that they hate lime as that they need a bigger than usual quantity of certain elements, particularly iron, magnesium and manganese. Since roots cannot eat but can only drink, these elements must be in the form of salts dissolved in water before the plant can make use of them. The presence of lime, however, turns these elements into an insoluble form, so that however much of them there may be in the soil the roots cannot take them up. The results is that the plant is starved of the foods it so vitally needs and soon develops symptoms of deficiency; the leaves lose their healthy green colour and turn pale yellow, and the plant sickens and stops growing. The chemicals called sequestrols contain iron and the other vital elements in what is known as a chelated form, which means that they cannot be made insoluble by lime, so the roots can take them up and the plant is properly nourished. The trouble is that when the elements are in such a readily soluble form they are very quickly washed away by rain, so the chemical has to be applied again and again. Fortunately there is no such problem in lime-free soil, where the iron and other elements are available in a natural form, soluble enough to be taken up by the plant roots but not so soluble that it gets washed away.

If you are lucky enough to have lime-free garden soil, you can grow a whole range of exciting and beautiful lime-hating trees and shrubs which are denied to less fortunate gardeners. A list of suitable kinds is given overleaf, on pages 91 to 93. Before turning to that list, let us consider what conditions are most suitable to ensure that the lime-haters you choose are given the best possible start and spend a long, happy and useful life in your garden.

Lime-hating plants evolved their particular characteristics in response to special conditions, and the more nearly you can reproduce those conditions the better. The mere absence of lime in the soil, though the first essential, is not enough in itself to make sure that the plants grow as well as they might.

Lime-free soils are otherwise known as acid soils, and acid soils generally contain a large proportion of organic matter, consisting mainly of the remains of dead plants. That is what gives heathland its spongy texture, and heathland is the natural habitat of very many lime-hating plants. The spongy nature of the soil enables it to hold large amounts of water, and so give the plants the cool, moist conditions that their usually rather thin and fibrous roots need to prevent them from drying out. Year after year a supply of new plant remains is added to the surface of the ground in the form of fallen leaves, which decay slowly, keep the soil moist and encourage the plants to produce surface roots, which in turn need a covering of yet more fallen leaves; and so the process continues.

To provide lime-haters with the right sort of home, therefore, the soil should have as much organic material added to it as possible, particularly near the surface. Peat is probably best for the purpose, but if you have a supply of leaf mould you can use that. Beware of garden compost for the purpose; it may contain lime, which is just what the plants do *not* want. After planting, mulch the surface with a good layer of leaf-mould or peat.

Azalea

SOME EASY LIME-HATERS

Apart from a few gentians and nearly all lilies (which are fit for the difficult rather than the easy garden), most lime-haters are trees or shrubs. Some of the best are listed below.

★ = evergreen. Height = maximum. E = Early. M = Mid. L = Late. Sp = Spring. Su = Summer. A = Autumn.

Name	**Flowering** Time	Colour	**Height** in.	cm	**Description**
★*Andromeda polifolia*	Sp	Pink	12	30	'Bog Rosemary'. Narrow leaves; waxy, urn-shaped flowers.
Azalea Ghent hybrids (*Rhododendron* section)	LSp	Various	96	240	The easiest kind, flowering when frost is over.
★*Calluna vulgaris* varieties	A	Mauve etc.	36	90	'Ling Heather'. Flowers freely over many weeks.

Name	Flowering Time	Colour	Height in.	cm	Description
**Camellia japonica* varieties	ESp	Pink etc.	144	360	Very hardy, though frost may damage open flowers.
**C. sasanqua* varieties	A-Sp	Pink etc.	120	300	Wide range of colour. Superb against any wall except east.
**C. × williamsii* varieties	W-Sp	Pink etc.	96	240	Clear coloured flowers over a long period.
**Cassiope lycopodioides*	MSp	White	2	5	Wiry stems; bell flowers; ideal ground-cover for lime-free soil.
**Chamaedaphne calyculata (Cassandra)*	Sp	White	36	90	Heath-like flowers on wiry, much branched shoots.
Clethra alnifolia	LSu	White	96	240	'Sweet Pepper Bush'. Richly aromatic flowers. Pink form too.
Cornus kousa	ESu	Cream	240	600	Small tree with large, handsome, creamy bracts.
C. sinensis	ESu	White	240	600	Chinese species with larger and showier bracts.
**Daboecia cantabrica*	Su-A	Purple, white	30	75	'St. Dabeoc's Heath'. Masses of flowers over very long period.
Disanthus cercidifolius	A	Purple	120	300	Insignificant flowers, but lovely soft crimson autumn leaves.
**Embothrium coccineum lanceolatum*	ESu	Brilliant crimson	360	900	'Chilean Fire Bush'. A glorious sight wreathed in fiery-red flowers.
Enkianthus campanulatus	LSp	Buff-yellow	96	240	Clusters of hanging bell-flowers Rich autumn leaf-tints.
**Erica arborea alpina*	ESp	White	96	240	'Tree Heath'. Splendid upright growth; scented white flowers.
**E. ciliaris*	Su-A	Rose etc.	12	30	'Dorset Heath'. Many varieties with rose, red and white flowers.
**E. cinerea* varieties	Su-A	Red etc.	12	30	'Bell Heather'. Purple, red, pink and white varieties available.
**E. scoparia* 'Minima'	ESu	—	24	60	Small green flowers but dense spires of apple-green foliage.

Daboecia cantabrica

Name	Flowering Time	Colour	Height in.	cm.	Description
Eucryphia glutinosa	Su	White	180	450	Shapely tree-like shrub. Feathery leaves turn red in autumn.
**Gaultheria miqueliana*	Su	White	8	20	Prostrate evergreen. Flowers followed by pearly white berries.
**G. procumbens*	Su	Pink	8	20	'Creeping Winter-green'. Valuable ever-green with red berries in winter.
Halesia carolina	LSp	White	300	750	'Snowdrop Tree'. Draped with clusters of hanging bell flowers.
Hamamelis mollis	W	Yellow	180	450	'Chinese Witch Hazel'. Cowslip-scented flowers all winter.
**Kalmia latifolia*	ESu	Shell-pink	96	240	'Calico Bush'. Flower-buds look like pink sugar-icing.
**Leucothoe davisiae*	ESu	White	36	90	Dark, glossy leaves and spikes of snow-white summer flowers.
**Lithospermum diffusum*	ESu	Blue	6	15	Prostrate shrub, producing many gentian-blue flowers.
Liquidambar styraciflua	Sp	Green	480	1200	'Sweet Gum'. Most brilliant scarlet autumn leaves, tiny flowers.
Magnolia denudata	ESp	Pure white	300	750	Lovely species with fragrant flowers before leaves appear.
**Pieris formosa forrestii*	Sp	Cream	96	240	Breathtaking pink-tinted young foliage each year.
**Rhododendron ponticum*	ESu	Mauve	210	300	The easiest species, flowering when frost is over.
**R.* in variety	Sp-Su	Various	180	450	Vast choice of medium and small varieties. Avoid tall kinds.
**Skimmia reevesiana*	Sp	Cream	36	90	Hermaphrodite, so flowers are always followed by scarlet berries.
Styrax japonica	ESu	White	180	450	'Snowbell'. Magnificent small tree; bell-like white flowers.

Gentian

Vegetables

BEFORE YOU decide to grow vegetables in your easy garden, think twice about it, and then think again. There is nothing easy about growing vegetables, if by easy you mean needing little work. In fact as soon as you start growing vegetables you will find that you have to spend much more time and effort in sowing, planting, transplanting, hoeing, watering, spraying and dusting.

True, there is great satisfaction in raising and eating your own vegetables. They are cheaper and fresher than the ones you buy, they taste better—at least to the person who grew them—and they are said to be better for you. That is why more and more people are growing their own, in spite of the extra work.

If you do not want, or do not have enough room, to make a special vegetable garden, you can plant a clump or two of the more decorative vegetables in your border, where they will enhance its beauty and give you something to eat as well. Globe artichokes are particularly good for this purpose, with their gracefully arching silver-grey leaves and elegant flower-heads, which are so delicious cooked and served with vinaigrette sauce or melted butter and cost a fortune to buy in the shops.

Asparagus can also provide a very attractive foil to other plants and flowers when it follows its succulent young shoots in the spring with its tall, fern-like foliage in the summer, turning to gold in the autumn. Even rhubarb (which may be stewed and eaten like fruit but is a true vegetable-garden subject) can make a striking border plant with its large, stately leaves on their blood red stalks. Apart from such permanent crops, which go on increasing and yielding food year after year and need no attention except tidying in the autumn and a sprinkling of fertiliser in the spring, it is possible to grow temporary decorative screens between different parts of the garden by planting runner beans; their long, hanging pods are as beautiful as their scarlet flowers.

Herbs can be grown at the front of the border. Parsley, thyme, marjoram and sage are easily raised from a sprinkling of seed, or plants may be bought quite cheaply. Rosemary, planted further back, makes a handsome evergreen bush.

POSITION OF SITE

If you are going to have a proper vegetable patch all on its own, as a separate plot within your garden, choose the most open site you can find, as far away as possible from the shade of buildings and trees. The risk of disease is much worse with vegetables in confined, shaded places; so if you cannot find an open spot, give up the idea of growing vegetables and save yourself trouble and disappointment.

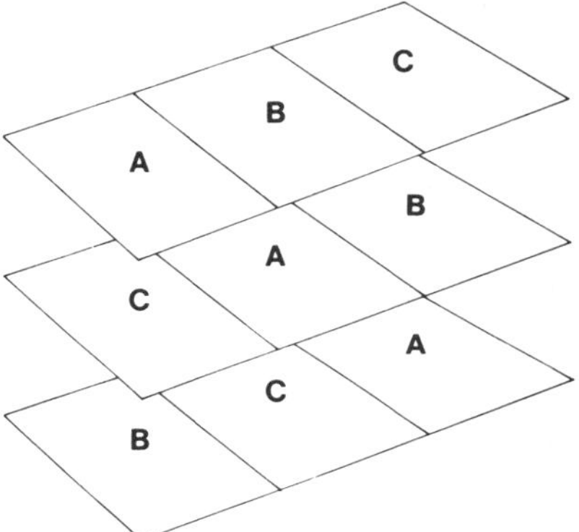

Rotation of crops plan

ROTATION OF CROPS

It is extremely important for easy management and for the health of your crops that you should not go on growing the same type of vegetable in the same place year after year. There are two reasons for this. First, different kinds of vegetables take up the various plant foods from the soil in different amounts, so they may become starved and show signs of mineral deficiency if constantly grown in the same place. Secondly a disease or pest, which attacks a special crop, may increase to plague proportions in the soil, if given that special crop to prey on year after year.

The easiest system for the amateur gardener with limited space is a three-year rotation. The way it works is this. Divide your vegetable plot into three equal parts. Section A has plenty of manure or compost dug into the ground and is used during the first season for growing things that love rich soil, such as peas, beans, celery, lettuce, onions, spinach and tomatoes. Section B is not manured but has fertiliser added; it is used for root crops such as carrots, beetroot, turnips, parsnips and potatoes. Section C is treated with fertiliser and is given a dressing of lime if necessary (see page 17); it is used for growing members of the cabbage family, which, besides cabbages, includes brussels sprouts, broccoli, cauliflowers, savoys and kale.

The second year section A becomes section C (given fertiliser and lime), section B becomes section A (given manure) and section C becomes section B (given fertiliser). The third year the original section A becomes B, the original section B becomes C, and the original section C becomes A.

In this way no crop occupies any section more than once in three years, with the result that the soil is improved instead of being impoverished and a build-up of pests and diseases is avoided.

VEGETABLE SOWING AND PLANTING GUIDE

E = Early. M = Mid. L = Late. Sp = Spring. Su = Summer. A = Autumn. W = Winter.

Vegetables sown under glass may be bought as plants. Stored means kept in dark frost-proof place; store roots in sand.

Kind of vegetable	Sow		Plant out	Distance				Can be used	
	In open	Under glass		Plants in.	Plants cm	Rows in.	Rows cm	Fresh	Stored
Artichoke (Globe)			L Sp	30	75	30	75	Su	
Artichoke (Jerusalem)			A or Sp	18	45	48	120		
Asparagus	M Sp		Sp	18	45	18	45	L Sp–E Su	
Aubergine		Sp	E Su	18	45	24	60	Su–A	
Beans									
Broad	A or Sp			8	20	30	75	E Su–L Su	
Dwarf French	M Sp–Su			8	20	18	45	M Su–A	
Runner	L Sp			12	30	60	150	Su–A	
Climbing French	L Sp			12	30	60	150	Su–A	
Beetroot	Sp–Su			4	10	14	35	Su–A	W–Sp
Broccoli (sprouting)	L Sp		M Su	18	45	24	60	Sp	
Brussels sprouts	Sp		E Su	24	60	30	75	A–Sp	
Cabbage									
spring	L Su		E A	18	45	24	60	L Sp–E Su	
summer		E Sp	Sp	18	45	24	60	Su–A	
winter	L Sp		M Su	18	45	24	60	LA–Sp	
Savoy	Sp		L Su	18	45	24	60	W–E Sp	
Calabrese	Sp		E Su	18	45	18	45	L Su–A	
Carrot	E Sp–E Su			4	10	12	30	E Su–A	W–Sp
Cauliflower									
winter	L Sp		M Su	24	60	24	60	E Sp–L Sp	
autumn	Sp		M Su	18	45	24	60	A–W	
summer		EA	Sp	18	45	24	60	M Su	
Celery		Sp	L Sp	8	20	48	120	A–W	
Cress (in trays)	Sp–Su	A–Sp						Any time	
Cucumber									
indoor		E Sp–A		30	75			Sp–A	
outdoor	L Sp	M Sp	E Su	30	75	48	120	Su–EA	

Kind of vegetable	Sow		Plant out	Distance				Can be used	
	In open	Under glass		Plants in.	Plants cm	Rows in.	Rows cm	Fresh	Stored
Kale	Sp		Su	24	60	24	60	A–Sp	
Leek	E Sp		E Su	8	20	18	45	A–Sp	
Lettuce	Sp–A			18	20	12	30	Sp–A	
Marrow		M–L Sp	E Su	30	75	60	150	Su–A	
Mustard (in trays)	Sp–Su	A–Sp						Any time	
Onion									
spring sown	Sp			8	20	18	45	Su	A–Su
Japanese	L Su			8	20	18	45	E Su	A–L Sp
sets			E Sp	6	15	14	35	Su	A–Su
Parsnip	E Sp			12	30	18	45	A–Sp	
Pea									
round seeded	A–E Sp			2	5	dwarf 24	60	E Su–A	
wrinkled	Sp–E Su			2	5	tall 48	120		
Peppers		Sp	E Su	18	45	24	60	Su–A	
Potato			Sp	12	30	24	60	M–L Su	A–E Su
Radish	E Sp–Su			1	2·5	8	20	L Sp–A	
Rhubarb	Sp		A–Sp	48	120	48	120	Sp–Su	
Seakale beet	Sp			9	23	14	35	Su–Sp	
Shallot			E Sp	8	20	12	30	E–M Su	L Su–L Sp
Spinach									
summer	E–L Sp			9	23	12	30	L Sp–A	
winter	L Su–A			9	23	12	30	A–Sp	
Spinach beet	Sp–Su			9	23	14	35	Su–Sp	
Swede	L Sp			12	30	18	45	A	
Sweet corn	L Sp	Sp		18	45	30	75	L Su	
Tomato		Sp	E Su	18	45	24	60	Su–A	
Turnip	Sp–Su			6	15	12	30	Su–A	W–Sp

THE EASIEST VEGETABLES

The following four pages (98 to 101) give a selection of some of the easiest vegetables for the amateur with limited space. They have been chosen because they take up little room, give a good return for your money and effort, stand up to cold weather, resist disease and pests and need little if any attention.

Asparagus (*Asparagus officinalis*)

Permanent crop. Though an expensive luxury in the shops, this is perhaps the cheapest and most trouble-free vegetable to grow. Buy one-year-old plants and that will be the last expense, except for an annual sprinkling of fertiliser, for a vegetable that will go on producing delicious crops every year for a lifetime. Choose well drained soil (mix in some sand if it is heavy), remove every scrap of perennial weed, and dig in plenty of manure or compost. In spring dig out a trench 6 inches (15 cm) deep and put in the young plants 15 inches (40 cm) apart along this. Spread out their roots carefully, cover them with 2½ inches (6 cm) of earth and tread this down firmly but gently, to avoid damage. As the plants grow, fill in the trench. Do not cut any shoots the following year. After that cut them each spring when they are about 4 inches (10 cm) above the ground; use a sharp knife and cut them off below soil level. After six weeks of cutting and eating, let the plants grow to their full height; leave them till the foliage turns yellow in the autumn and then cut them down. A sprinkling of fertiliser early each spring and an occasional weeding is all the attention asparagus needs.

Broad beans (*Vicia faba*)

Section A. These are the hardiest and most trouble-free of all the beans. In mild districts they may be sown in the autumn to stand the winter; in cold places sow them in early spring. The seed should be planted 2 inches (5 cm) deep and 9 inches (25 cm) apart in a zigzag double row. In most places the plants are self-supporting, but in windy gardens string taken round the row about 18 inches (45 cm) above ground level and fixed to stakes driven firmly into the earth at each corner will ensure that no damage is done. If blackfly appears, pinch out the growing tips of the plants. Pick the pods while the beans inside are young and tender, and before they have developed hard skins.

Broad beans

Beetroot

Beetroot (*Beta vulgaris*)
Section B. You need never be without beetroot if you sow at the right times. Choose a globe kind; the long-rooted one grow bigger but coarser. Sow 1 inch (2·5 cm) deep, in rows 12 inches (30 cm) apart, so sow very thinly; then you will not need to thin seedlings out till they are big enough to use. The ones left to grow on should be about 4 inches (10 cm) apart. Gather them while they are still young and tender. Make three more sowings in late spring, early summer and midsummer. The last sowing will give you roots which can be lifted in the autumn. Take off the leaves an inch or two above the crown and either store the roots in boxes of sand in a frost-proof place or cook, skin and pickle them. In that way you will have fresh beetroot throughout the summer till early autumn, and stored or pickled beetroot for the rest of the year.

Broccoli

Broccoli (*Brassica oleracea botrytis cymosa* cultivars)
Section C. Of all the cabbage family, sprouting broccoli is probably the easiest to grow and the most rewarding. There are three kinds: purple-sprouting, white-sprouting and green-sprouting (otherwise known as Calabrese). All are sown during spring, about ¾ inch (2 cm) deep in short rows in a seed-bed. As soon as the seedlings are about 4 inches (10 cm) high, transplant them to their final quarters, 18 inches (45 cm) apart, with a distance of 2 feet (60 cm) between rows. Tread the soil very firmly round them after planting. You should be able to cut succulent shoots from the green-sprouting kind in the summer and autumn, and from the purple- and white-sprouting ones in the spring.

Carrots

Carrot (*Daucus carota*)
Section B. The top favourite root vegetable, this may be sown little and often over a three-month period, from early spring to early summer. Choose a short-rooted variety, sow very sparingly and thin to 2 inches (5 cm) apart. Pull and use carrots while they are young and sweet. If maggots of the carrot-fly are a nuisance, rake soil insecticide into the soil before sowing; or try growing carrots between rows of onions, which the fly is said to hate because of the smell. Lift remaining roots before hard frosts start and store in sand in a frost-proof place for winter use.

Leeks

Leek (*Allium porrum*)
Section A. This is perhaps the hardiest of all vegetables and will stand the harshest winter. Sow in a rather thick row, ½ inch (1·5 cm) deep, in early spring. Leave the seedlings rather overcrowded, so that they grow drawn and spindly. In the summer, when they are about 6 inches (15 cm) high, it is time to transplant them. Make a row of holes 6 inches (15 cm) deep, and 8 inches (20 cm) apart. If you have room for more than one row, space them 12 inches (30 cm) apart. Use a dibber or a thick stick about 1½ inches (4 cm) in diameter. Lift the young plants carefully from their seed bed, drop one in each hole so that just the tip protrudes, and water it in. Do not fill in any soil. When you dig up the leeks in the winter, you will find a length of sweet, white, juicy stem below the surface where the hole was.

Lettuce

Lettuce (*Lactuca sativa*)
Any section (preferably A). If you can only grow one vegetable, make it lettuce. No other crop gives so much for so little; and there is no comparison in flavour or texture between a crisp, newly cut, home-grown lettuce and the average flabby article bought from a shop. There are basically three types of lettuce, two with hearts and one without. The one without, known as the loose-leaf or salad-bowl type, is useful commercially because, having no pretence of crispness, it does not break up in transport, no matter how roughly it is handled. Since the only transport we are concerned with is the short distance from garden to kitchen, there is no point in growing this type. Of the two with hearts, the upright cos-lettuce is rather more difficult to grow. That leaves the round cabbage type, which in turn is divided into soft-leaved butterhead varieties and crinkly-leaved crisp ones. The butterhead is the usual limp kind sold in shops, so grow the crinkly leaved type, which is much nicer to eat. Sow a small amount every two or three weeks—½ inch (1·5 cm) deep, in rows 12 inches (30 cm) apart—from spring to late summer. That will give you fresh lettuce from early summer to late autumn. If you sow hardy winter kinds in late summer, you can have spring lettuce too. With cloches or a cold greenhouse, you can sow during autumn and winter and so extend the lettuce season.

Onion (*Allium cepa*)
Section A. There are three ways to grow onions. The cheapest is from seed sown in the spring. If you sow rather thickly and gradually thin to about 6 inches (15 cm) apart you can use the thinnings as spring onions in salads. The disadvantage is that in many places the disgusting white maggots of the onion fly will eat out the middle of all spring-sown onions and wreck the crop. Insecticide powder raked into the soil before sowing helps, but it is fairly expensive stuff, and many people disapprove of chemical gardening, especially with food crops. The second way to avoid the problem is by sowing one of the modern hardy sorts in late summer when the flies are no longer a nuisance. The seed is more expensive, but the time, effort and insecticide saved more than compensate; besides if you leave the plants unthinned till the following year you will get earlier spring onions from the thinnings. The third way is the most expensive but gives least trouble: it is to buy sets (small bulbs) and plant them 6 inches (15 cm) apart, in rows 12 inches (30 cm) apart, in early spring. The fly will not bother them and you can lift and store them in late summer.

Onions

Radish (*Raphanus sativus*)
Section C. The easiest and quickest of all crops, radish will produce usable roots within a month of sowing. A member of the cabbage family, it may be grown in the same section. It is so quick, however, that it can be sown between slower things and used before they need the space. Sow a small amount of seed ½ inch (1·5 cm) deep, every two weeks from early spring to late summer and you will have juicy radishes from mid-spring till the winter frosts start. Sow thinly and start gathering the biggest roots first, leaving the smaller ones to swell out. Even if you have no vegetable garden, you can sow a pinch or two of radish seed whenever there is a vacant patch in a border or bed, to give a quick crop from otherwise wasted ground.

In addition to summer radishes there are the much bigger winter kinds, with black or rose-coloured skin and delicious white flesh. Do not sow these till after midsummer. They are hardy enough to stand the winter out of doors and give a welcome crop when there are few fresh vegetables about.

Radish

Fruit

Bush apple tree

Standard apple tree

Perhaps like many other amateur gardeners you dream of sitting under your own fruit tree eating your own fruit. Better let it remain a dream unless you are willing and able to put in a great deal of work. You get a better type of fruit in dreams—or for that matter in the shops—than the miserable, scabby maggot-infested specimens that the average garden produces in real life.

The sad fact is that the amount of work needed to grow fruit well is second only to the amount needed to grow vegetables; but while you can grow better vegetables than you can buy, you can usually buy better fruit than you can grow. The reason is that in order to get clean crops, free from blemishes caused by the many pests and diseases that attack fruit, the professional grower has to go in for an elaborate programme of regular spraying which would be beyond the resources—in time, money and patience—of the amateur gardener.

If, in spite of all that, you decide you want to have a go, the following notes may help.

TREE FRUIT

Apples

Apples are the most commonly grown, and are available in a large number of different varieties: early and late, cooking and dessert. If you can only grow one, make it a self-fertile kind; if more, choose ones that will fertilise each other; your supplier will advise. Buy trees on dwarfing root-stocks, so that they do not grow too big.

The bush is the most usual shape, where the main stem is quite short and the branches start close to the ground. Many people choose the bush type because it does not spread very far and can be planted as little as 9 feet (2.75 metres) apart.

The standard, on the other hand, has a main stem about as high as a tall man to the point where the branches start and because of its wider spread must be planted no nearer than 15 feet (4·5 metres) apart. So, of course, you cannot have as many standards as bushes in a given space. There is, however, a problem if you plant bush trees in grass, as a semi-decorative feature: you cannot mow under them without knocking into the branches. For easy gardening, better plant standards, because you can stand upright under the branches while mowing without braining yourself.

If the apples are not to be planted in grass, and so there is no problem about mowing, try one of the trained forms; these take up little space and because they are much smaller than the full-sized kinds it is easy to reach every part of them for the purpose of pruning, spraying and fruit-picking.

THE DWARF PYRAMID has become increasingly popular during recent years. Many can be planted in quite a small space, 4 feet (1·2 metres) apart. It takes a good deal of time and skill to create this shape, so do not attempt it yourself. Buy four-year-olds already shaped, and keep them in trim by cutting back new end growth on branches (but not the central leader) to five leaves as it becomes woody in late summer. Laterals are cut to three leaves and side-shoots from these to one leaf. In spring cut back the central leader to half the previous year's growth. This will build up a system of closely spaced blossom buds and give a lot of easily picked fruit on a compact plant.

THE CORDON is even more compact, and can be planted as little as 3 feet (1 metre) apart. It is fixed at an angle of 45° to ground level and needs to be supported on horizontal wires. Cut back side shoots to three leaves when they become woody in late summer; secondary growth after that may be cut back to one bud in autumn or winter. Do not prune the main stem leader till the spring; then it can be cut back to as little as ½ inch if it has reached the top wire. In this way a single stem with knobbly fruiting spurs is built up over the years.

THE ESPALIER is a tree trained on a wall or on wires, and consists of a central upright stem with horizontal branches on each side. Each of these branches is pruned in exactly the same way as a cordon.

All of these trained forms of tree have the advantage that they will produce a lot of fruit in a very restricted space; but they do need a considerable amount of pruning to keep them in shape. If you cannot be bothered, grow standards, which need little or no pruning. If they grow so big that some of the fruit is out of reach, get a gathering bag on a pole; you push the rim under the stalk and the fruit drops into the bag.

Sometimes, in spite of all your efforts to keep it restricted, a tree will grow too strongly, so that it makes a large quantity of leaves and shoots but not enough flowers and fruits. One way that can be very successful in reducing this over-vigorous growth is to perform a small operation called bark-ringing. With a sharp knife you cut away a strip of bark from one side of the main stem below where the branches start. Two or three inches under this, on the other side of

Pyramid apple tree

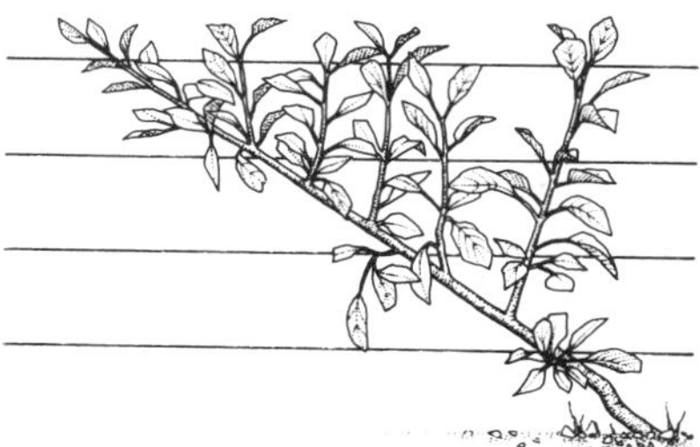

Cordon apple tree

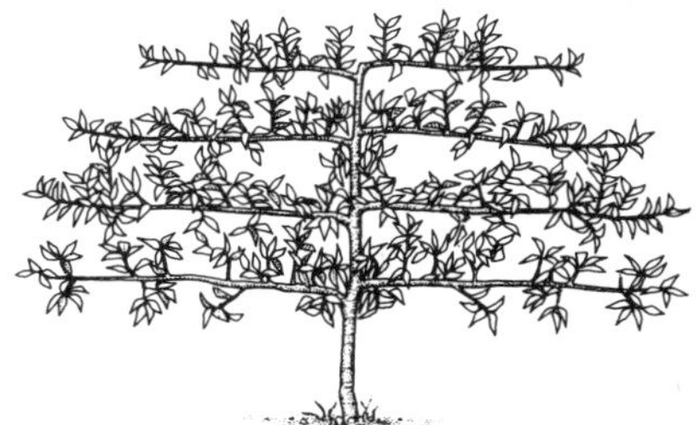

Espalier apple tree

the main stem, cut out another strip of bark. The removal of this bark will interfere with the flow of sap and cause the over-enthusiastic growth of the tree to slow down.

At least a hundred different pests and diseases can attack apple trees. However only a few are really serious and these can usually be kept under control by a programme of spraying. There are many chemicals available which will kill active pests during the growing season but the easiest way to keep them under control is to kill the eggs before they can hatch out. For this purpose the trees may be sprayed, during the winter when they are leafless, with a fruit-tree winter wash, based on tar-oil or DNOC and petroleum. Spray very thoroughly, so that every part of the tree is covered. Not only will this kill the eggs of dozens of pests, from aphids to apple-suckers to winter moth, but it will destroy the spores of some troublesome diseases such as blossom-wilt and powdery mildew; it will also clean off moss and lichen. Winter washes are very powerful things, and must never be used after the buds have begun to swell in the early spring, otherwise you will kill the tree as well as the pests. Also be careful not to get drops of the spray on growing plants, or you will damage them. Cover them with newspaper.

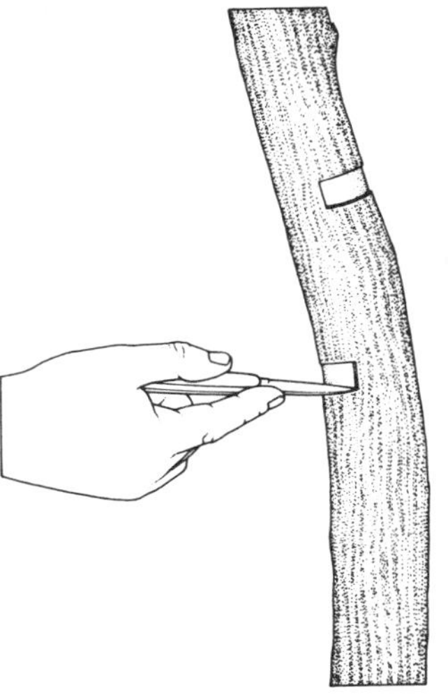

Bark-ringing to reduce growth

The most widespread and destructive disease is scab, which can ruin the fruit. The best way to deal with this is to spray in the spring with a suitable fungicide (lime-sulphur is commonly used, but modern ones based on such chemicals as benomyl are safer) at four stages: green bud, pink bud, petal fall and when the fruitlets begin to swell. This anti-scab spray may be mixed with an insecticide so that while you are preventing disease you are destroying pests as well.

One of the worst pests is the winter moth, a very prolific mother whose caterpillars can make such a mess of apple trees in spring. She cannot fly and so has to crawl up the trunk of the tree in the autumn to lay her eggs, which she deposits around the buds, so that when her loathsome offspring hatch out in the spring they have a ready-made meal as the buds start to open. If you spray with a winter wash as advised, most of the eggs will be killed, but if you have not sprayed, or want to make doubly sure, fix a grease-band round the trunk in late summer; this will trap the female moth as she tries to crawl across it and she will come to a sticky end.

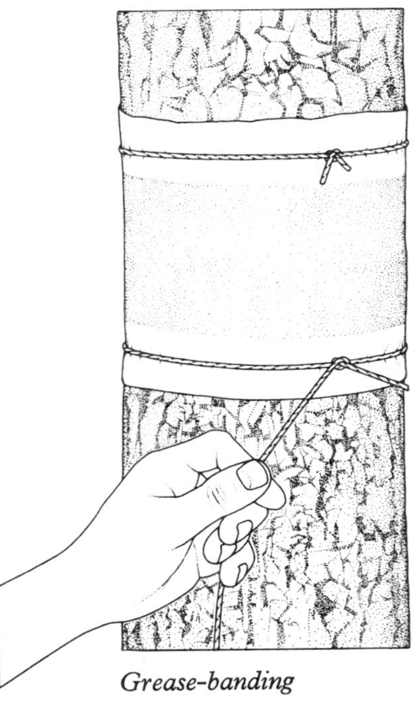

Grease-banding

Pears

Pears are the next most commonly grown tree-fruit. They can be grown in any of the same forms as apples and are subject to the same kinds of trouble, so they should be treated in exactly the same way. The most marked difference is that they form fruit-spurs more readily and therefore need less pruning.

Plums

Plums cannot successfully be trained in restricted forms, because they react badly to pruning. Grow them as standards or half-standards and do no cutting except to remove dead or diseased wood.

Peaches

Peaches are much hardier than was once thought and can be grown as bushes or standards in the open garden. They produce beautiful fruit when trained against a sunny wall, but to do so properly takes endless time and labour, and so cannot by any stretch of the imagination be considered easy gardening.

Cherries

Cherries are very beautiful but very difficult. The bitter morello kind, which makes delicious jam and is used in the best cherry brandy, can be grown against a wall; it even thrives on a north wall, where very few other things flourish. The sweet kinds of cherry, however, are very demanding in their requirements. They not only need plenty of space, because it is impossible to keep them dwarf, but they are self-sterile, and have to be planted near others, according to an elaborate system of fertility rules, if they are to produce fruit.

Figs

Figs can be grown in a fan shape against a wall. Cut back some branches each winter to encourage new ones to grow from the base.

SOFT FRUIT

In a small garden this is usually more rewarding than tree fruit. Soft fruit does not take up so much room; it gives a bigger return for the space it occupies; it is easier to manage; and it does not suffer from so many pests and diseases.

Strawberries

Strawberries are the favourites among all soft-fruit and if grown well give the best crop. Unfortunately they are also subject to more troubles than the rest. However, most of these troubles are not too bad if you stick to two simple rules.

Rule one is this: *always buy certified plants from a reputable supplier*. This means that they have been examined and officially declared to be free from the virus disease that causes infected plants to produce miserable crops of inferior fruit.

Rule two is this: *never grow strawberries in the same place for more than two years running*. Nature never intended strawberry plants to live long. Their natural life-style is to send out runners which produce new young plantlets. As these grow in size and vigour they take the energy from the parent plants, which—worn out with bearing so many offspring and carrying fruit as well—soon become old, withered and useless. It is better then to dig them up and put them on the compost-heap, where they will turn into valuable humus-forming material, than to let them linger on in the hope that they will recover their lost youth. They never will. This does not mean that you have to keep on buying new plants. They are provided for you free. Choose the best runners as they appear in early summer and peg them down with bent wire into pots of compost sunk into the soil. They will be well rooted by midsummer, when they can be cut from the parent plant and moved to a new bed.

Layering strawberry into pot with wire 'hairpin'

Cultivated strawberries are of two types: those that fruit once in the summer only and those—called perpetual-fruiting—that go on producing fruit till late autumn. If possible grow some of each. If you have room for only one kind grow the perpetual-fruiting type, which will give you strawberries for five months of the year instead of a few weeks. Take no notice of people who tell you this type is inferior. They are simply ignorant. The latest perpetual-fruiting varieties give superb fruit.

The best place for strawberries is the vegetable garden. Mix plenty of manure, compost or peat into the top layer of soil, and rake in a dressing of general fertiliser. You can plant strawberries in the spring, but it is much better to do so in the summer or autumn—the earlier the better, so that they can make new roots before the winter. Plant 18 inches (45 cm) apart, in rows 30 inches (75 cm) apart. Make small mounds of soil in the centre of the planting holes and sit the plants on them with their crowns just level with the surface of the ground. Fill in the earth, make it firm, and finish with a good watering.

Cultivation consists largely of destroying weeds. Commercial growers do this by using chemical herbicides. Only the least poisonous ones are available to the amateur, and you can use these if you follow the instructions *exactly* (see pages 122 and 123). It is safer, both for your plants and for you, to pull out weeds as they appear or to hoe them off at ground level. Be careful not to damage the roots of the strawberries; weeds cause less trouble than damaged roots.

As fruit begins to form, tuck straw or plastic under the plants to prevent the berries getting dirty. Or there are special strawberry mats which are much quicker and easier and can be used again and again.

The fruit will need to be protected from birds. Plastic netting stretched over a metal or wooden framework and held down at the edges by stones or bricks will do the job. The best thing is to have two strawberry beds going at once, one containing one-year-old plants and the other two-year-olds. Each year a new bed is planted with fresh runners, and at the end of the season the two-year-old lot are scrapped.

Strawberry mat to protect fruit

Black currants

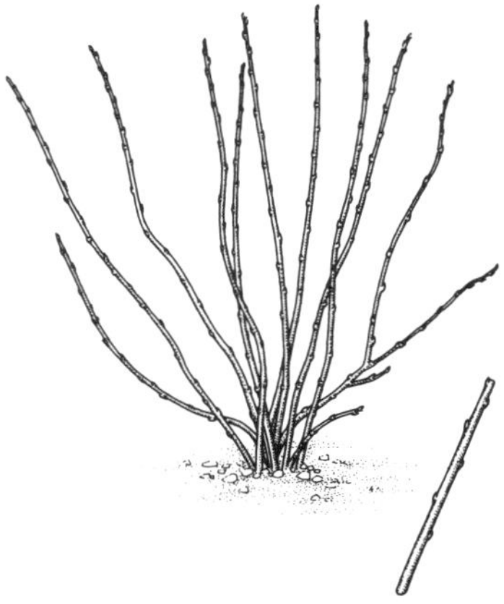

Blackcurrant bush and cutting

Black currants are another rewarding crop, so long as you buy your plants from a reputable supplier whose stock is certified as free from disease. Firmly refuse any offer of free plants or cuttings from friends; such plants may be carriers of the virus disease called reversion, which distorts leaves and reduces the crop drastically. Plant in good soil which has been enriched with plenty of manure or compost and given a sprinkling of general fertiliser. Planting can be done at any time in the autumn or winter. Allow a distance of about 5 feet (1·5 metres) between the bushes, and put them in rather deeply. Make the earth very firm round them and cut the shoots down hard so that only two buds are left above the ground. This will encourage new shoots to grow from under the soil during the first season. That autumn cut out any inward-pointing or weak shoots and leave the rest intact. The following year this wood, which by then will be one year old, will carry the first crop of berries. Each year after that, as soon as the fruit has been picked, cut back at least a third of the dark-coloured older wood, leaving the lighter coloured new season's growth to replace it. The purpose of pruning is to keep getting rid of as much old wood as possible (none of it should be more than four years old) and to replace it with young shoots which will bear fruit when they are one year old. Any overcrowded young shoots should be cut out after leaf-fall; they can easily be used as cuttings to make new plants if the unripe tip is removed and the shoot cut to about 8 inches (20 cm) in length just below a bud. Leave all the buds on the cutting and plant it firmly in the ground with only the tip showing. By the following autumn it should have grown several shoots and be ready for transplanting. Abnormally swollen buds on branches in early spring are a sign of infestation by big-bud mite, which ruins crops and spreads disease. Pick off the swollen buds and burn them. Some control of big-bud mite is possible if you spray with lime-sulphur in the spring just before the first flowers open.

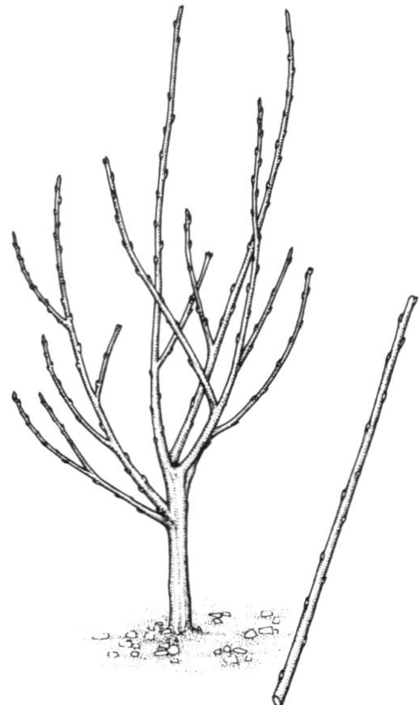

Redcurrant bush and cutting

Red currants

Red currants bear fruit on the old wood, and are usually grown as bushes on a 'leg', a bare main stem, about 8 inches (20 cm) high. Plant in the same sort of soil, and at the same distance apart, as black currants. Cut back each branch to four or five buds. The following winter remove any overcrowded or inward-pointing shoots, shorten the branch-leaders by about a half, and cut back side-shoots to one bud. In subsequent years build up a framework of nine or ten main branches and prune side-shoots back hard to form fruiting spurs. From time to time remove old played-out branches and replace them by vigorous new shoots. To make new bushes, take cuttings about 12 inches (30 cm) long, remove all buds except the top four and plant firmly about 3 inches (8 cm) deep. Birds will get your fruits, and perhaps peck out buds in the winter, unless you protect the bushes with netting.

White currants

White currants are simply a form of red currant and are treated in exactly the same way.

Gooseberries

Gooseberries bear fruit both on new wood and on spurs from old wood. Grow them on a leg, as with red currants, and prune them in much the same way. Net against birds.

Raspberries

Raspberries are best grown in a row and trained against wires, stretched between firmly anchored posts. Some people use two single wires, at about 2½ feet (75 cm) and 5 feet (150 cm) above ground level, and tie the cane to them. Others find it easier to have a pair of parallel wires, 12 inches (30 cm) apart, strung between cross-pieces fixed to the supporting posts 4 feet (120 cm) above the ground; the canes can then be tucked between the wires instead of having to be tied. Plant the canes 18 inches (45 cm) apart in ground enriched with manure or compost. After planting cut them down to about 8 inches (20 cm) above ground level. During the first season they will grow. During the second season they will fruit while new canes are growing. After that summer-fruiting varieties have old canes cut out and new ones trained to the wires each year. Autumn-fruiting raspberries have all canes cut down to ground level in early spring.

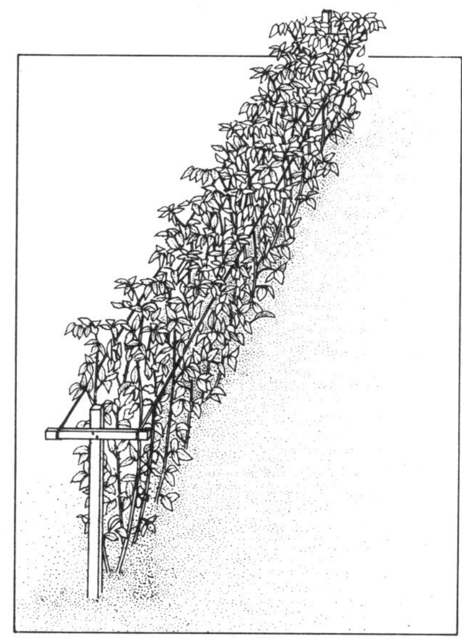

Raspberry wires

Blackberries and Loganberries

Blackberries and Loganberries are more vigorous relatives of the raspberry. They must be tied firmly to single wires; they are too heavy and sprawling to be held in place by twin wires.

Cut it Out

A GREAT DEAL of aimless lopping and chopping goes on in gardens every year, because people have been told, or have read somewhere, that they ought to be doing something called pruning. As a kind of occupational therapy, to make people with time on their hands feel that they are doing something useful, it may have its value; but as far as the plants are concerned, more often than not it does a great more harm than good. The first rule of easy and successful pruning is this: *never prune at all unless you have a very good reason for doing so.* There is a natural balance, or at any rate there should be, between the parts of a plant that you can see above the ground and the invisible part below. In normal circumstances the roots of a tree or shrub occupy just about the same amount of space as the branches and leaves. So if you cut a plant back hard it will react by trying to restore the balance. As quickly as possible it will send out more shoots in order to have as much branch and leaf area as the roots were intended to support. That is why a pruned branch tends to produce two or more shoots instead of one, because that is the quickest way for it to get as much new leaf area as possible. So before you cut anything, remember that generally speaking *pruning does not reduce growth but increases it.* After continually being cut back, a tree or shrub will become a thicket of crowded shoots; that is why clipped hedges become so thick. But crowded growth, apart from being less pleasing to the eye, is much more liable to disease, just like human beings in overcrowded conditions. Plenty of light and air are needed for healthy growth.

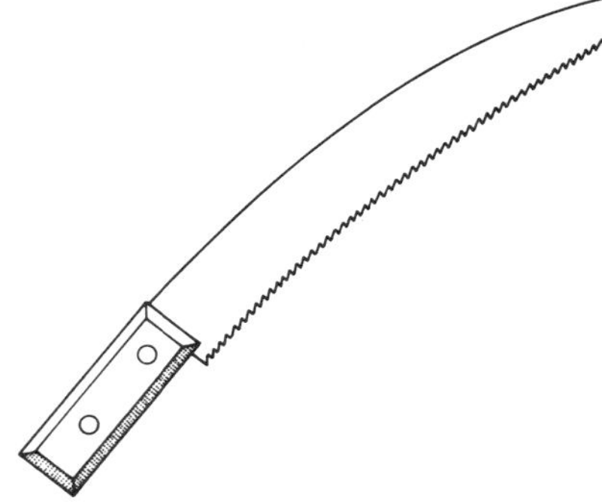

Coarse-toothed pruning saw

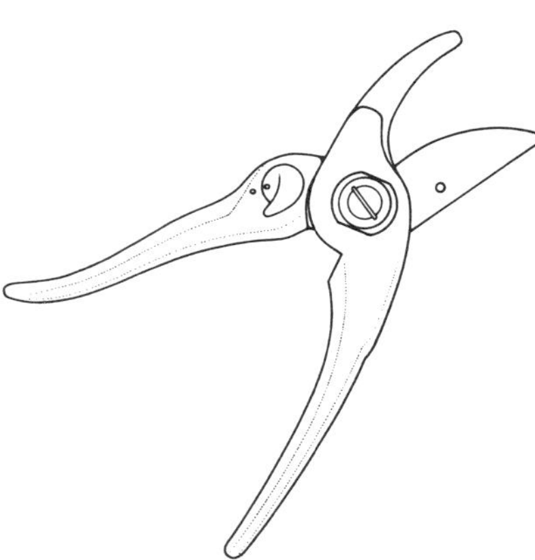

Pruning secateurs

In any case, cutting in itself makes a plant more liable to infection, because an open wound is easily invaded by disease. A ragged cut makes matters worse. On the other hand, for cutting off branches of any size, a pruning saw is needed, and to reduce effort this should have coarse teeth because fine ones get clogged with sap. But coarse teeth, though less effort to use, make irregular, easily infected cuts.

All pruning is a kind of surgery, but removing branches thick enough to need a saw is major surgery and should only be done if it cannot be avoided. Unfortunately this form of surgery cannot be performed in germ-free hospital conditions, so the cut must be treated as soon after being made as possible, to reduce the risk of infection. The best way is to take a really sharp knife and go over the surface of the cut to remove irregularities and pare it to a smooth finish, which will be much less open to invasion by disease. Be careful to direct the knife away from yourself, or you may finish up by paring your own hand.

As an added precaution, you can paint the cut with a good waterproof paint. There are special ones sold for treating pruning-wounds, but ordinary paint left over from decorating the outside of the house is perfectly adequate for the job. Often it is recommended that white paint should be used, but white has no magic property that makes it better than other colours. Use anything to hand—purple if that is what you happen to have. It may look a bit out of place, but it will soon be covered by the growth of new tissue, and if all goes well the wound will before long have disappeared from sight under fresh bark.

However, things should not normally be allowed to get to the stage where thick branches have to be removed. What you should aim at is trimming rather than amputation. Try to avoid having to prune any shoot that is more than one year old. If you cannot cut it easily with one stroke of the secateurs you have let it get too big.

Some experts still use a knife for pruning, but they are a dying breed. Modern secateurs will give excellent results with much less trouble. There are two types. With anvil ones the blade strikes a soft metal plate after cutting through the wood; they are somewhat cheaper, but more likely to bruise the shoot. With the best knife-cut ones the blade has a slicing action and so is less likely to do damage. In dealing with branches that are hard to reach, long-handled pruners make the job much easier.

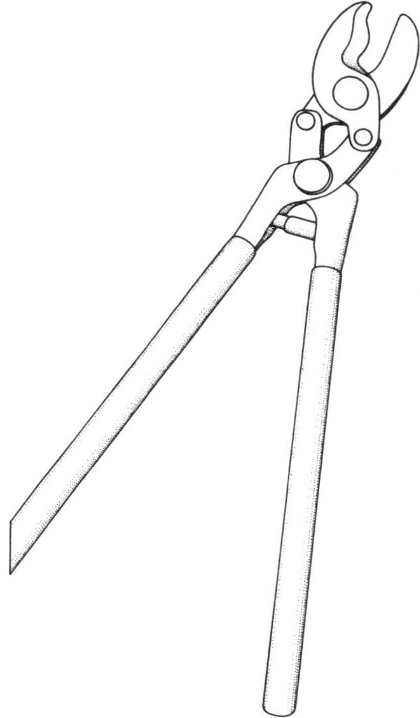

Long-handled pruners

An important rule for good pruning is always to use sharp tools; they not only make the job quicker and less tiring but give better results, because clean cuts heal more rapidly than torn or bruised ones caused by blunt blades. So if your secateurs are at all blunt, sharpen them with a fine-grade oil-stone, or even a household sharpener designed to put a good edge on table-knives; electrically powered ones are a joy to use. Blades that have become loose or out of alignment should be reset by an expert. If your secateurs are worn out, or the blades badly notched by use, or if they are simply of the old-fashioned kind with two blades, which squeeze instead of slicing, throw them away and buy a new pair, or get someone to give you one. You should always put a reasonable value on your time and not waste it trying to make do with second-rate equipment. Use good tools and save the pruning-cuts from frayed edges and yourself from a frayed temper.

The most important principle, to save both yourself and your trees and shrubs from trouble, is this: *never leave any wood that is bound to die after pruning*. When removing a branch do not allow a stump—otherwise known as a snag or a hat-peg—to remain; it will not grow, and anything that will not grow must eventually decay. The trouble is that the decay is likely to spread down into the live wood and carry infection through the whole tree or shrub, weakening or even killing it. So cut the branch to be removed right back to the point where it starts, leaving no stump, so that the surface of the cut is flush with the main stem. First saw the underside of the unwanted branch upwards for an inch or two, to ensure that when it is sawn through from the upper side it does not suddenly crash down, tearing a strip of bark with it. If the branch to be removed is heavy, it may be best to saw it off in sections. That will avoid strain, and make tearing unlikely.

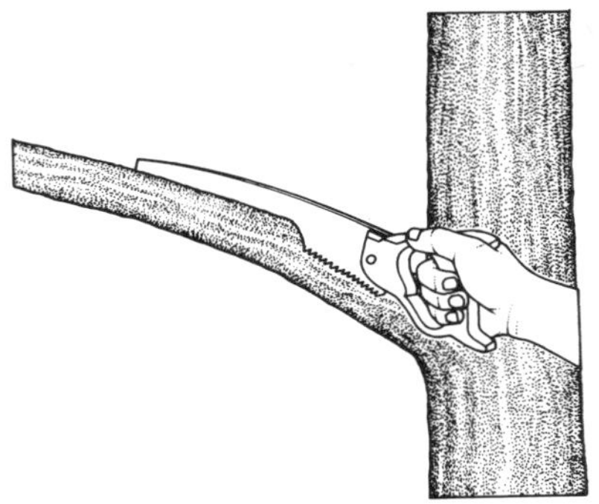

Wrong way to prune a branch leaving a 'snag'

The same principle as that described for large branches thick enough to need a saw also applies to shoots thin enough to be cut off with secateurs. Never leave any wood that juts out beyond a joint or does not end in a bud. It will only die back and may become infected in the process. Even a very small piece of surplus shoot left beyond a bud is a potential disease-carrier.

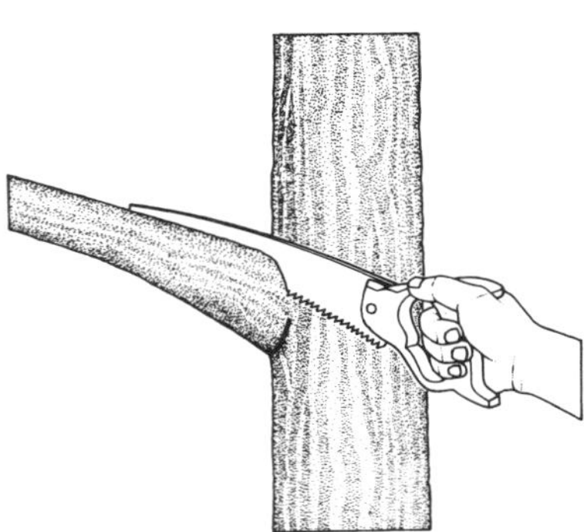

Correct way to prune a branch

That is why everything should be done to help the cut to heal over as quickly as possible, and healing tissue (or cambium, as it is called) can only form over living cells. To keep these cells alive needs sap, and sap can only flow through a line leading to growing points, not through stumps left out of the sap-stream like drift-wood landed high and dry on a beach when the tide goes out. In order to make sure that all useless wood which will not carry sap is removed, the slope of each pruning-cut must be just right. If you cut some way above a bud, as we have seen, the surplus wood will die. If you prune just above a bud but make the cut slope downwards towards the bud you will still have a tapering snag of wood which cannot heal over. If you do not slope the cut but prune straight across the shoot at right angles you will still have a small portion of wood on the side opposite the bud which may not heal. But if you slope the cut so that on the bud side of the shoot it is just above the bud and on the opposite side it is just below, the wood will remain alive and soon heal over. Do not make the slope of the cut too steep, or the bud may dry out and wither. Then the bud below it will become the growing point and you will have created between the dead and the live buds just the kind of stump that you want to avoid.

There is one other pruning instrument in common use: the garden shears. Most of the time they are used for hedge-trimming—which is, after all, a form of pruning—but they are also very useful for trimming low-growing plants, such as heather, which form clumps and would take too long to prune with secateurs.

The pruning of roses is a special art, and is dealt with in the appropriate section on pages 75 and 76. Pruning in the fruit garden is also an art in itself and is dealt with on pages 102 to 109. This section deals with the pruning of ornamental trees and shrubs and looks at why and how it is done.

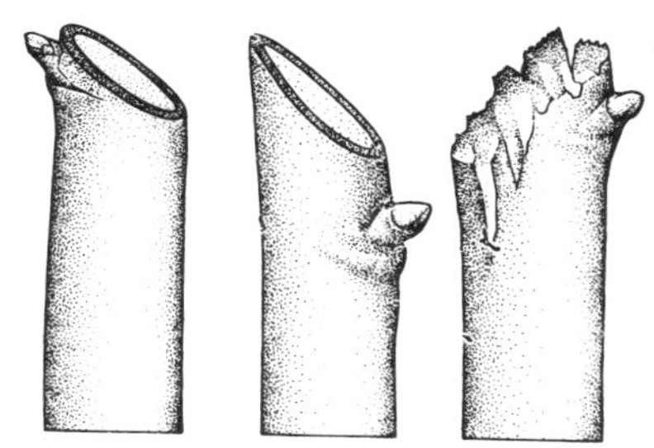

Wrong ways to prune

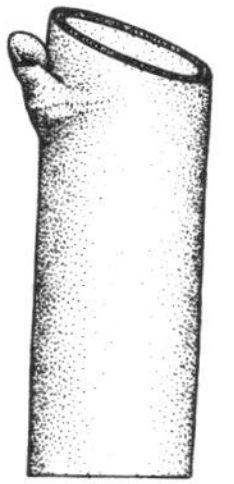

Correct way to prune

There are four good reasons and one bad reason for pruning. The bad reason is to restrict the growth of something that grows too big, in order to fit it into a garden that is too small. It would be much better to get rid of such a specimen and plant something of more suitable size. Mutilating large things to try to make them small takes a lot of time and labour and the results are horrible. The four good reasons are: (a) to remove dead or diseased wood, (b) to help achieve a pleasing shape, (c) to keep the plants tidy, and (d) to make them produce the best possible display of blossom, fruit or foliage, according to the kind of plant and the particular attraction for which it is grown.

In removing dead or diseased wood it is very important to cut back to healthy growth. If there is a brown stain in the wood where you cut it, that means that there is an infection at that point; so you must cut it back still farther, if necessary again and again, till the wood is clean and shows no staining. Only then can you be confident that you have removed all the possible source of infection.

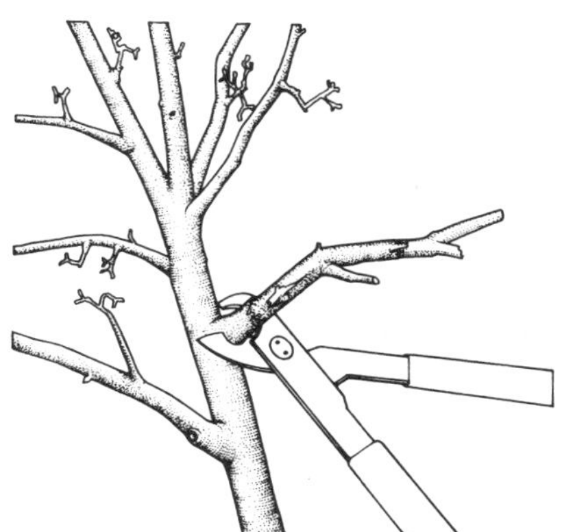

Removing dead wood

After every bit of dead and diseased wood has been cut out, the next thing is to improve the shape of the plant by pruning away all overcrowded shoots, especially those growing inwards towards the centre; that, as we have seen, makes the plant not only more attractive but healthier, by letting in light and air.

Sometimes a very coarse shoot will appear, growing much faster than the rest and threatening to take over completely. Such a growth, called a 'water-shoot', is best cut right out at its base before it starves the other shoots of sap and ruins the shape of the plant.

The final reason for pruning, to produce a better display, only applies to a limited number of shrubs, which fall into two types.

The first is made up of those that flower on the previous year's wood. Since any wood older than that will never flower again, such shrubs tend to become more and more leggy, the new growth for carrying next year's flowers appearing at the end of bare branches which have had their day. The following year that new growth will in turn be old and bare, and a further crop of new shoots will need to grow from the end of it to carry next year's flowers.

Pruning is perfectly simple if you remember that with shrubs of this type *branches are too old at two years of age*. The thing to do, therefore, it to cut them back as soon as they have finished flowering to two or three buds or shoots from the point where they start. In this way you will keep up the supply of young shoots and keep down the amount of useless old wood. The shrub will remain compact and you will be able to enjoy the flowers at eye-level instead of from below. Some of the shrubs that do well with this treatment are *Buddleia alternifolia*, *Spiraea* × *arguta* and species of *Deutzia*, *Kerria*, *Philadelphus*, *Ribes* and *Weigela*.

The second type of shrub that benefits from hard pruning is the kind that flowers in late summer or autumn on new wood produced during the same year. In this case the wood only starts growth that spring and is no more than six months old when it bears flowers. It therefore has a good deal of growth to make in a very short time.

With shrubs of this type, *shoots are too old at the age of one*. The correct way of pruning, therefore, is to cut them hard back to one or two buds from where they join the older wood. Do this as soon as the buds start to swell in the spring so that the greatest possible amount of new growth is made before flowering-time comes. Among shrubs that respond well to this treatment are *Buddleia davidii*, *Caryopteris*, *Ceanothus* (deciduous kinds), *Ceratostigma*, *Fuchsia*, *Leycesteria*, *Passiflora*, *Santolina*, *Spartium* and many late-flowering species and hybrids of *Spiraea*.

Apart from the two types just mentioned, most shrubs do best without being pruned.

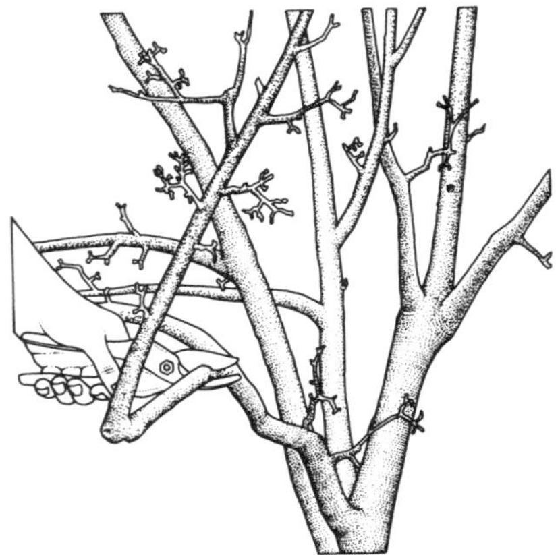

Removing overcrowded and inward-growing shoots

Removing shoots growing too long

Spiraea

Defeating Weeds

AT THE beginning of this book (page 2) a list was given of the tasks that take the most time and effort in the average garden. At the top of that list came weeding, which gardeners find more tiring, boring and generally discouraging than any other job.

Whatever can be done to reduce and lighten the burden of weeding will therefore do more than any other single thing to create an easy garden. Weeds are a state of mind. They are simply plants growing where you do not want them to grow. What makes them weeds is not the nature of the plants themselves but your attitude of antagonism towards them. After all, every plant that grows started from a weed somewhere; even our most cherished garden beauties may be a great nuisance in their native habitat, where they interfere with the efforts of gardeners to grow foreign plants which are weeds somewhere else. There are four things you can do about weeds. You can ignore them, prevent them, fight them or use them.

Bindweed

IGNORING WEEDS

This may at first sight seem to be the easiest form of gardening, but pretty soon the ignored weeds will turn your garden into a jungle. Then you will have the task of trying to turn that jungle back into a garden again, and that is the hardest job of all. So by taking too easy a line with your weeds to begin with, you finish up with a lot of extra work.

Couch-grass

The trouble is that native weeds are much better adapted to the conditions in your garden than the foreigners which you have planted there. So the weeds are bound to win if they are given a fair chance. That brings us to the first rule of successful weed control. To win the battle against them always remember this: *never give weeds a fair chance.*

If you do, they will soon take advantage of their superior adaptability and your plants will be the losers. Weeds harm cultivated plants in three ways: (a) they rob them of space, air, light, food and water; (b) in many cases their roots send out chemicals that spoil or prevent the growth of other things near them; and (c) they provide a breeding ground for pests and diseases, which do them little harm but which may seriously damage the less robust cultivated plants.

Ignoring weeds, then, is not an effective way of dealing with them. It may relieve you of work to begin with, but it will cause much more labour in the end.

PREVENTING WEEDS

The second way of tackling weeds, by preventing them, is the most effective and labour-saving one, and should be used wherever possible. The main method is to occupy the ground with other plants so that the surface is completely covered and weed-seeds do not get a fair chance of falling on bare earth, or if they do they are prevented from germination and denied food by the ground-cover plants. It is then the weeds that become the intruders, and like all intruders they are placed at a disadvantage by the closed ranks of the existing inhabitants. This method of preventing weeds is dealt with in more detail in the section *Ground-cover plants*, on pages 46 to 51.

A modern method of weed-prevention by chemicals is dealt with later in the present section, on page 122; and an old-fashioned but still effective (and more natural) way, by means of mulching, is discussed on the same page.

Ground-elder

Nettle

FIGHTING WEEDS

The third method of dealing with weeds, by fighting them, still has to be used in many cases, especially where bare-earth gardening is necessary or unavoidable, as in fruit and vegetable gardens.

To fight successfully, you must first know your enemies, so some are pictured on these pages. Simple outline drawings of young seedlings are included in some cases, so that you can recognize and destroy them at the earliest stage. Weeds are of three kinds. In descending order of nastiness, these are: perennials, biennials and annuals.

PERENNIAL WEEDS

There are two sorts of perennial weeds: those with and those without runners. Of the two, those with runners are much more difficult to control. Four of the worst are pictured here: Large Bindweed (*Calystegia sepium*), Couch-grass (*Agropyron repens*), Ground-elder (*Aegopodium podagraria*) and Stinging Nettle (*Urtica dioica*). In their case, the runners are below ground and consist of rooting parts, or rhizomes, which spread rapidly through the soil during the growing season and can give rise to a new plant at any point along their length, so that within a terrifying short time there are whole strings of plants above ground to show where the runners have spread below.

Another pernicious weed that multiplies itself by runners at an alarming speed is the Creeping Thistle (*Cirsium arvense*), which has vicious little spines. These drive themselves into your skin if you are unwise enough to try to pull up the plant without first putting on gloves, and are very difficult to remove; but if you leave them in they can cause a painful rash. Unlike many runner-propagated weeds, which produce little or no seed, the creeping thistle if allowed to flower makes large quantities of small seeds, surmounted by silky white fluff which enables them to be carried quite long distances by the wind to colonize fresh ground. Coltsfoot (*Tussilago farfara*) is even worse in this respect because the seeds are finer, fluffier and more numerous. In many ways the worst weed of all, if you are unlucky enough to be plagued by it, is the Horsetail (*Equisetum arvense*), a 'living fossil' of a very ancient type that inhabited the earth long before flowering plants appeared. Not only does it spread sideways but it can send its rhizomes down into the subsoil to a depth of a yard (1 metre) or more; in addition, it develops a kind of underground tuber, which acts as a winter food store for the new rhizomes that sprout in the spring; and as if that were not enough it has a primitive extra method of reproduction by means of spores, a fine brown powder carried on the wind, each of its millions of tiny particles capable of growing into a new plant. Among other weeds spreading by underground runners are Japanese Knotgrass (*Polygonum cuspidatum*) a pushful member of the dock family and its cousin the Sheeps' Sorrel (*Rumex acetosella*), which thrives in acid soil. The problem with all of these weeds that spread by underground runners is that by attacking them you may actually help them to spread. They have a mixture of strength and weakness which they exploit to great advantage in order to extend their territory and increase their numbers. The rhizomes are strong enough to drive their way through the hardest soil, but brittle enough to break easily into several pieces, and each piece may contain a tiny bud which enables it to grow into a new plant. So if in trying to dig them out you leave any bits behind in the soil, you will be creating more weeds than you started with.

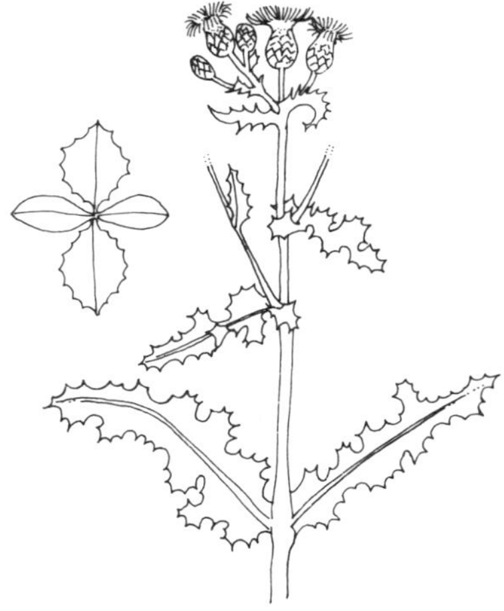

Creeping Thistle

Coltsfoot

The Creeping Buttercup (*Ranunculus repens*) belongs to another class of spreading perennial weeds, those with runners above instead of below ground level. On the whole these are easier to deal with, because at least you can see where they are. Sometimes they can be destroyed by burying them deeply, since unlike underground rhizomes their runners are incapable of pushing their way through the soil;

so they stay where they have been buried and suffocate. Among non-runnering perennials that are difficult to deal with are weeds such as the Lesser Celandine (*Ranunculus ficaria*) which produce small storage organs called bulbils. These are bulb-like structures which are really packaged plants in miniature, containing food and moisture for the baby plant and protected by a thick skin. Unlike rhizomes and runners, which if dug out and laid on the ground during dry weather will shrivel through loss of moisture, bulbils can last for a long time because they are very efficiently protected from drying out. If left on the ground they will soon send out roots into the soil, and by expansion and contraction these roots will pull the bulbil down into the earth.

Finally there are perennials that have no runners or bulbils but rely for their survival on building thick, deep-probing roots. In winter the tops die down, but in spring buds burst into growth and the plant grows bigger and more difficult to cope with. Weeds of this kind include Docks (*Rumex crispus* and *Rumex obtusifolius*) and the Dandelion (*Taraxacum officinale*). Digging out these deep, fleshy roots is not easy, and any pieces left in the soil are likely to regenerate and form new plants.

Ways of dealing with difficult weeds are given in the following pages (120–123). Meanwhile remember: *never trust weeds*. They have become very clever at survival over their long history, and one of their cleverest tricks is to look dead after you have dug them up, so that you do not bother to remove them. Never believe them. The tiniest dead-looking bit may contain enough life to start a new plant while your back is turned. So always take away every scrap of perennial weed that you have unearthed, and burn it. *Tidying up is much less work than weeding.*

BIENNIAL WEEDS

These are the ones that last for two seasons and then die. They germinate the first year and develop a thick root or stem which becomes packed with plant food. This provides for new growth in the second year, during which it produces flowers and seeds; after that it has no further purpose in life and is too exhausted to continue living in any case. There are very few troublesome biennials. The commonest are probably Wild Carrot (*Daucus carota*) and the Burdocks (*Arctium* species). They should be removed during their first year, before they have a chance to build up strength for flowering.

Chickweed

ANNUAL WEEDS

Though there are some winter annuals, which germinate in the autumn and winter and remain as dormant seed throughout the summer, the vast majority are summer annuals. These germinate in the spring, grow and flower and produce seed during the summer, die down in the autumn and remain as dormant seed throughout the winter.

Groundsel

Annuals are much easier to deal with than perennials as single plants, because they are shallow rooters and do not live long enough to become hard to dig out. In the mass, however, annuals can be very troublesome indeed. Being entirely dependent on seed for the survival of the species they make it in vast quantities; one plant of Shepherd's Purse (*Capsella bursa-pastoris*) can produce five thousand seeds. Each of those seeds can lie unnoticed in the ground for weeks, months or years before it germinates. Hence the old saying: *one year's seeding is seven years' weeding*. The secret of dealing with annual weeds is to destroy them before they produce seed. For safety's sake that means before they flower, since a few early blooms can open unnoticed and produce seed before the main flowering takes place. Three of the worst annual weeds are illustrated, so that you may recognize them and get rid of them before they have time to flower and produce seeds. They are: Chickweed (*Stellaria media*), Groundsel (*Senecio vulgaris*) and Annual Meadow-grass (*Poa annua*), all fairly common.

CONTROLLING WEEDS BY CULTIVATION

Annual Meadow-grass

The most usual way of dealing with annual weeds is to chop them off with a hoe. They can also be dug into the ground, where they will rot down to form humus, and so enrich the soil. Be careful to bury them completely; if they are left on the surface where the light can get at them they may root and grow again. Remember that it is only annual weeds which can be safely buried. Most perennials, as we have seen, can form new plants from the tiniest pieces of rhizome, so when you dig them up it is most important that you should get out every little bit. *Dig gently*. The rougher you are in your treatment of them, the more likely you are to break them up and so increase the number of new plants. Every piece of rhizome should be removed and burnt; in fact it is best to burn the green top growth as well, since that is quite capable of forming roots if left in the soil.

However careful you are, it is likely that you will leave some bits behind, and very soon, if the conditions are favourable to them, they will sprout and send up new shoots. In order to do so they must use up some of their own body cells. Later, when their leaves open out, those cells will be replaced by new ones manufactured by the leaves from air and sunlight, and then the new plants will start building themselves up and increasing in size; so you will soon have more and bigger weeds than if you had left them alone. The secret of defeating them is to remove the new shoots as soon as they appear above the ground, while the underground parts are giving up more of their body substance than they are getting back. If you continue to chop off every shoot with a hoe before the leaves have time to open out, you are bound to win; every time this happens the roots shrivel a little more, till in the end they are too exhausted to try again. Overleaf, on pages 122 and 123, you will find information on how to deal with weeds by the latest chemical means. This may seem like the last word in easy gardening, requiring no effort at all. Unfortunately that is not quite true. Chemicals have to be applied with great care, they are not cheap, and there are some dangers in their use, so if you can manage to conquer weeds by cultivation, so much the better.

CHEMICAL CONTROL

The most modern way to deal with weeds is by means of chemical weedkillers. These have been developed greatly in the last few years and they can, if understood and used correctly, take nearly all the effort and backache out of weeding. If incorrectly used, they can be a menace not only to weeds but to cultivated plants—and to people. Some weedkillers, known as 'total herbicides', destroy all plant life indiscriminately, and can therefore only be used on uncultivated ground and on paths and terraces (so long as you do not want to grow plants in them). The cheapest and most commonly used is sodium chlorate, which can kill the toughest of weeds if applied at a rate of 2 ounces to a square yard. It will prevent all plant growth for a year or more; it should not be used where there are tree-roots below the surface, or it will be washed down and may damage or even kill them; and when it dries it can become explosive, unless you use the kind that has been treated to make it safe. Other weed-killers are more selective in their action. They include 'pre-emergence herbicides', applied before the seeds you sow germinate, and 'post-emergence herbicides', applied after the seedlings appear above the ground. Some are 'contact herbicides', which kill as they touch; others are 'translocated herbicides', which are absorbed by the plant and kill it from the inside. The table opposite shows some of the chemicals available under various brand names and what they are used for. To make sure of applying liquid herbicides only where you want and not splashing them on cherished plants, get a 'dribble-bar' to fit on the spout of your watering-can; this can be used nearly at soil level and delivers exactly the right dose.

Weeder bar attached to watering can

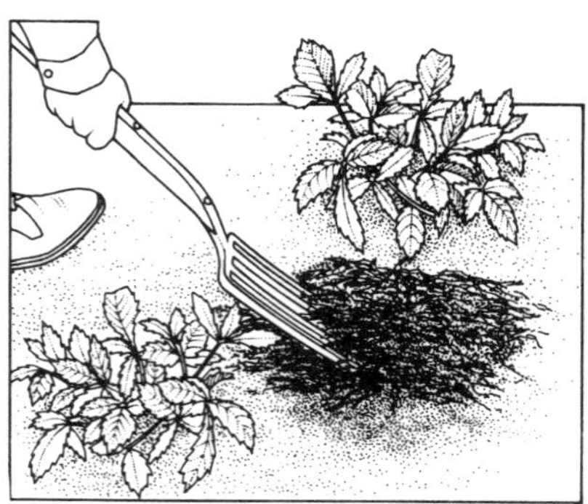

Mulching around and between plants to suppress weeds

MULCHING

One of the simplest ways to suppress weeds is to mulch the surface of the soil round your plants with a good layer of peat, leaf mould or compost. The odd weed that does appear will make surface roots into the mulch and so be much easier to destroy.

USING WEEDS

Finally, you can encourage annual weeds to grow on waste land, or on temporarily unoccupied ground, by feeding them with a high-nitrogen fertilizer such as ammonium sulphate, which causes plenty of soft growth. When well grown, cut them and add them to the compost-heap (page 21), where they will quickly rot down into excellent soil-enriching material. If not enough weeds grow, sow left-over seed; or you can buy special green-manure seed, such as rape or tares, for the purpose.

CHEMICAL CONTROL OF WEEDS

The herbicides listed below are available under various brand names. They can seriously damage cherished plants if allowed to drift on to them. It is best to apply them through a watering can with a weeder-bar fixed to the spout. Do not use a fine spray; the tiny droplets may be carried a considerable distance by even a light wind. *Always follow the instructions on the pack exactly*. Many herbicides are highly dangerous, not only to plants but to pets and people.

Place	**Weeds**	**Herbicide**
Uncultivated or waste land	All kinds	Sodium chlorate
	Shrubby growth	2,4,5-T + 2,4-D
	Coarse grass	Dalapon
Paths and drives	All kinds	Simazine, MCPA and aminotriozole.
	Annual and germinating weeds	Simazine, diquat and paraquat.
Lawns	Most lawn weeds	Mecoprop, dichlorprop and 2,4-D
	Moss	Mercurous chloride (calomel)
Shrub borders*	Established weeds	Diquat and paraquat
	Seedlings	Dichlobenil, applied in spring
Perennial borders* and annual beds	Germinating weeds	Propachlor
Vegetable garden*	Germinating weeds	Propachlor
Fruit garden	Established annuals	Diquat and paraquat
	Germinating weeds	Dichlobenil, applied in spring.
	Grass weeds	Dalapon

* Particular care needed not to contaminate garden plants.

Defeating Pests and Diseases

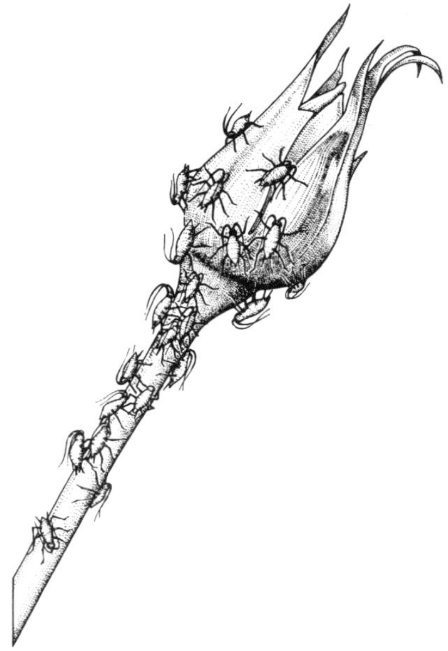

Greenfly on shoot and calyx behind rose-bud

READING THROUGH a list of symptoms of the many troubles that can befall garden plants is rather like studying a medical dictionary. Pretty soon you come to believe that you are suffering from every complaint in the book. The important thing is to cultivate an easy mind and not to worry too much; otherwise gardening will become a misery instead of a pleasure. If you take too seriously all the warnings by the manufacturers of garden insecticides and fungicides about what will happen unless you constantly spray and dust with their products, you will never know peace of mind; and your garden, instead of being pleasantly perfumed with the scent of flowers, will smell like a chemical factory.

It is an impossible task to get rid of all the bugs and beetles and things that live on plants, so the best thing to do is to stop trying. In any case, nature usually strikes a balance to prevent any pests from getting out of hand. When the pest threatens to reach epidemic proportions, other bugs appear for which it provides a meal; as these bugs multiply, others arrive to eat them; and so it goes on, each pest being controlled by some other creature to which it is food. So the gardener has at least as many friends as foes, with the result that if you take a live-and-let-live attitude and leave pest-control to nature, things on the whole tend to put themselves right, *so long as your plants are strong and healthy*. Pests and diseases are nature's way of getting rid of the unfit. That is why they particularly attack those plants that are least able to resist them. The best way, therefore, to avoid troubles is to build up the resistance of your plants. First, choose only the strongest. Eliminate weaklings. They are a waste of your time. Your garden should be a home for healthy plants, which can look after themselves, rather than a hospital for sick ones, which demand constant attention.

Plants, like human beings, need four things for healthy growth: space, fresh air, light and food (but not too much). Give them those things and they will be able to ward off most ills most of the time. Prevention is not only better than cure but easier too. Do *not*, however, over-protect plants by constantly spraying them with pesticides before troubles appear; that would be like dosing yourself with medicine before you were ill, and would increase the resistance not of the plants but of the bugs and germs that attack them.

Occasionally prevention will fail and you will have to use a remedy instead. The descriptions in this section will help you to recognise some of the commonest troubles as soon as they occur, so that you can deal with them before they become too serious. On page 127 is a table telling you what to do about some common pests and on page 131 one giving remedies for some of the more usual diseases.

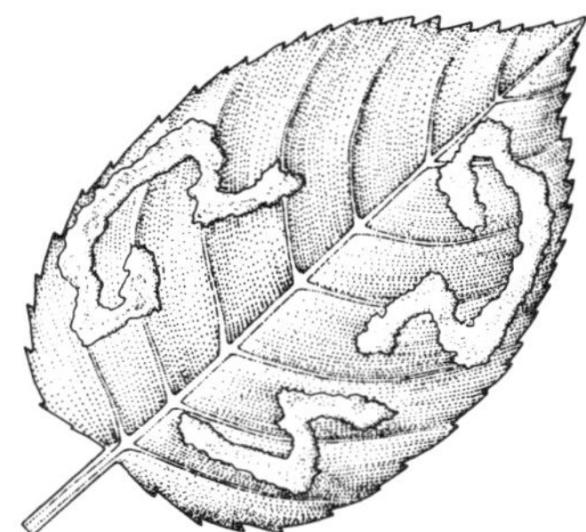
Leaf-miner causing silvery blisters

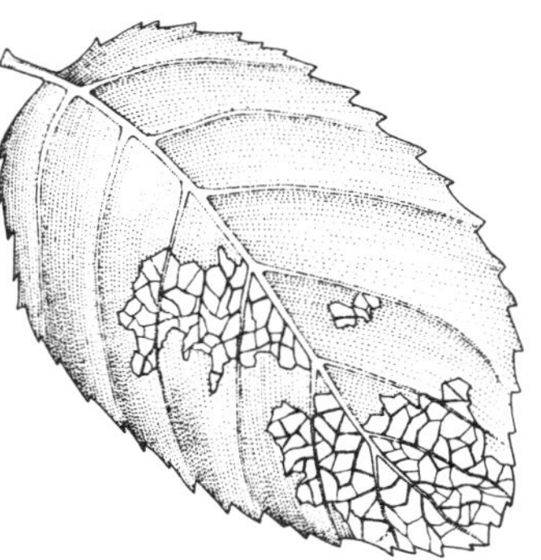
Slugworm skeletonising rose leaf

PESTS

These can be divided into two main kinds: sucking pests and biting pests. The suckers have no means of chewing and so cannot eat solid food; they penetrate the skin of plants with a thing like a hollow needle, which they insert into the sap-stream, and through which they draw up the plant juices just like somebody sucking a drink through a straw. The biters, on the other hand, have jaws of various kinds with which they can eat solid parts of plants; some can chew anything, skin and all, and so leave holes, while others can only manage the soft inner tissues, and so leave tunnels and blisters.

Sucking pests

APHIDS are by far the commonest of these. They are often called greenfly, though there are also black ones, grey ones, brown ones and pink ones. They have winged and wingless forms, they can reproduce with or without sexual intercourse, and they multiply at a fantastic rate. Experts who work that sort of thing out have calculated that within a few generations the descendants of one single greenfly would completely cover the globe if they all survived. Aphids attack every kind of plant and particularly like soft young growth.

THRIPS are those tiny 'thunder-flies' which puncture leaves and flowers, causing mottling and distortion.

RED SPIDER MITE is a pest of hot, dry conditions. It infects the undersides of leaves, turning them a pale rusty colour, and is worst in greenhouses.

WHITEFLY is a creature like a tiny white moth, which also has a scale-like form. It exudes sticky secretions which become black with a fungus called sooty mould.

Biting pests

LEAF MINERS are only able to chew the soft middle parts of leaves between the upper and lower skins. They eat their way along, leaving tunnels as they go.

SLUGWORMS also can only chew soft stuff. They eat the green tissue of rose leaves, leaving a skeleton of veins.

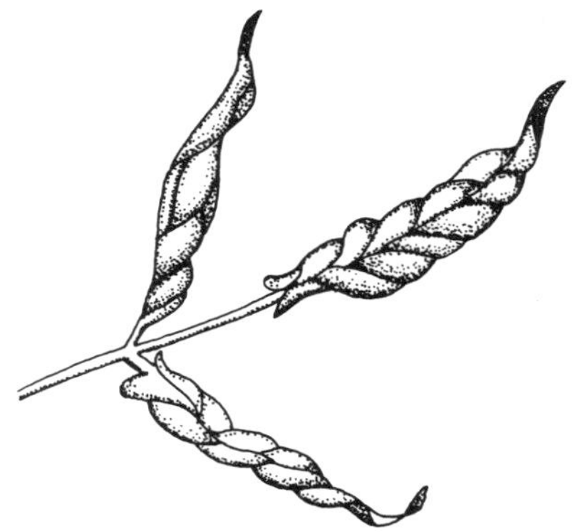
Sawfly grub causing leaf-roll in roses

SAWFLIES are of many different kinds and do considerable damage to a wide range of garden plants. The young white grubs eat their way through various parts according to their species, from the fruit of apples and plums to the leaves of gooseberries and currants, which they can quickly reduce to shreds. The one shown here is the rose sawfly, the grub of which rolls a rose-leaf tightly round itself, causing the leaf to cease to function properly.

CATERPILLARS of all kinds can do an enormous amount of damage in every part of the garden. They mostly eat leaves and have a tremendous appetite. The reason is that they need to grow very fast during their brief life-span between hatching out of a tiny egg and turning into the butterfly or moth or whatever other adult creature they are destined to become.

CUTWORMS are caterpillars that live in the soil and eat through the stems of plants at ground level. One of these cutworms with a hearty appetite is capable of destroying a whole row of seedlings in a single night, after which it hides underneath a stone or clod of earth to sleep off its heavy meal.

WIREWORMS, LEATHERJACKETS, MILLEPEDES and CHAFER GRUBS are other soil pests that can do great damage by eating the roots, stems, tubers and other underground parts of a wide variety of plants.

SLUGS and SNAILS are perhaps the most widespread and serious of all soil pests. They generally hide under stones, in crevices or under rubbish during the day and come out at night to eat whatever they can find in the vegetable line. They are particularly fond of the very young and the very old—that is to say young seedlings and old decaying leaves—because they are so soft and easy to chew; but failing such soft delicacies they will eat anything they can find—stems, roots, leaves, flowers and fruit. They are worst in damp weather and usually show where they have been by leaving a slimy trail behind them.

RATS AND MICE can do great damage, particularly in the vegetable garden, where they carry off newly sown peas and beans to feed their young.

BIRDS are on the whole the gardener's friends, eating all kinds of pests. They can, however, become a nuisance by pecking up seeds and seedlings.

PESTS AND THEIR CONTROL

There are so many pesticides on the market, under such a variety of trade names, that only a small selection can be given here. They are relatively safe, so far as is known at present, *as long as the manufacturer's instructions are strictly followed.* There are three kinds: (a) contact poisons, which kill by touch, (b) stomach poisons, which kill the pest after it has eaten part of the plant on which the poison has been sprayed, and (c) systemic poisons, which are absorbed into the plant's sap-stream and kill the pest when it tries to take a drink of sap. At any time the chemicals listed here may be superseded by newer and more effective ones, or withdrawn because they have been found to be dangerous. Note: for those worried about chemical poisons, each entry gives a safe alternative to begin with, though it may not be the most effective.

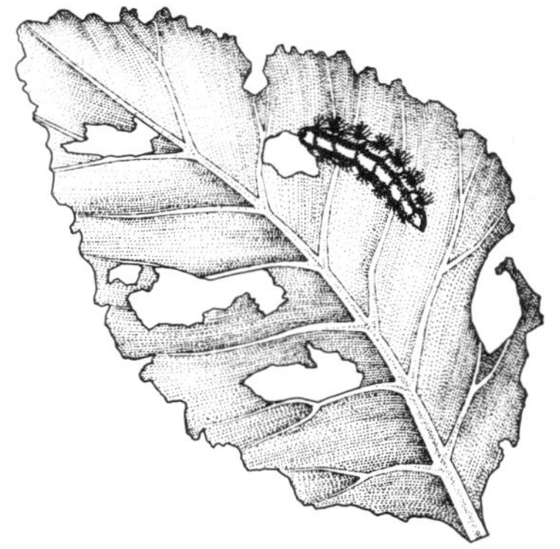

Caterpillar eating leaf

PEST	**CONTROL**	
	Safest	**Most effective**
Sucking		
Aphids	Derris	Systemic, e.g. formothion, BHC, malathion, pirimicarb.
Red spider	Derris	Chlorfenson, dimethoate, formothion, malathion
Thrips	Derris Pyrethrum	BHC, dimethoate, malathion
Whitefly	Pyrethrum	Resmethrin, BHC, dimethoate, malathion
Biting		
Leaf miners	Pyrethrum Remove leaves	BHC, diazinon, malathion, trichlorphon
Slugworms	Derris	BHC, malathion, trichlorphon.
Sawflies	Derris	Fenitrothion, BHC, dimethoate, trichlorphon
Caterpillars	Derris Pyrethrum	BHC, carbaryl, malathion, trichlorphon
Soilpests	Track down and squash	BHC, bromophos or carbaryl dusts.
Rats and mice	Soak peas etc. in paraffin	Put down warfarin bait each day until it is not eaten
Birds	Stretch black thread or place wire netting over seeds.	In this case most effective is the same as safest.

DISEASES

The air in your garden is full of millions upon millions of disease-germs. Yet very few plants show signs of disease. Why is that? The answer lies in natural resistance. *Normally a healthy plant is stronger than a disease germ.* If its health can be maintained, the plant will usually win.

When disease strikes, therefore, the first thing to ask yourself is whether anything is wrong with the way the plant has been grown. Is it overcrowded? Undernourished? Overfed? Too wet? Too dry? Very often putting right unsuitable conditions will remedy the trouble. If, however, the plant has become a miserable weak specimen, dig it up and replace it with a healthy new one. Do not waste your time nursing half-dead plants. Most plant complaints come into one of three categories: functional disorders, fungus diseases and virus diseases.

Mildew on chrysanthemum leaf

Functional disorders

These include all conditions where there is no identifiable disease present but the plant is not growing properly. More often than not it is suffering from deficiency of some vital food, but sometimes the trouble is caused by an excess of something that it either does not need at all or requires only in minute quantities. The nutritional needs of plants are somewhat complicated and too much of one element may prevent the plant from being able to absorb another. That is why it is unwise for amateur gardeners to attempt to make up their own artificial fertilizers by mixing together different chemicals. Failure to get them thoroughly blended in exactly the right proportions may result in poisoning the plants. So always buy ready-mixed compound fertilizers which are little if any more expensive and are easier to use. The symptoms of food deficiency in plants include stunting of growth and thin leaves, which may have dead patches especially round the edges and often look pale. Lack of some minerals, however, may turn leaves blue or bronze, gold or red; sometimes the veins will be darker or lighter than the rest. Try adding a mixed fertilizer to the soil, but be careful not to use more than it says on the packet. Or spray the leaves with a foliar feed, which sometimes brings a dramatic improvement. If the trouble persists, get the Horticultural Adviser from your local authority to come and have a look and, if necessary, arrange for a soil analysis.

Apart from deficiencies in diet because of the lack (or sometimes the toxic surplus) of certain minerals, the main cause of functional disorders in plants is trouble with their water supply. When the roots of a plant are taking up as much water as is passing through the leaves, things are in balance and the plant is firm and healthy. When more water is being given off by the leaves than the roots can supply, the plant flops and the leaves go limp. That can happen just because the weather is very hot, in which case the plant will recover at night; watering may help, so long as it is thorough (surface dribbles are worse than useless) and permitted by law (it may be banned during a drought). If the plant does not properly recover, but remains limp, the roots are not functioning properly. They may have shrivelled through lack of moisture, in which case the soil needs more organic matter, or been drowned through too much water, in which case the soil needs draining.

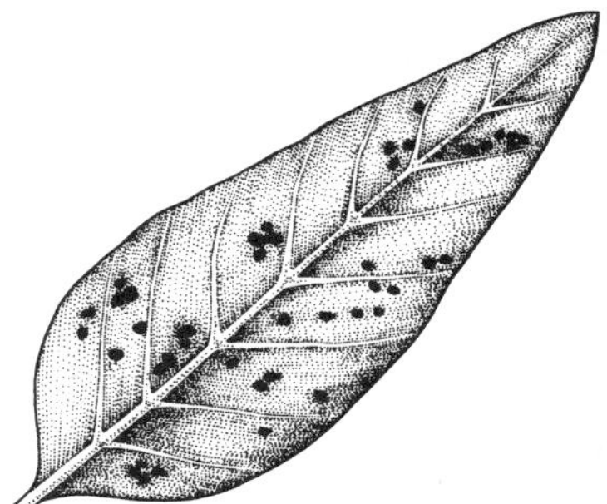

Rust on antirrhinum leaf

Fungus diseases

POWDERY MILDEW is one of the commonest diseases and attacks every kind of plant—trees, shrubs, perennials, annuals, vegetables and fruit. It appears as a white, powdery covering and can spread very quickly. A damp atmosphere encourages mildew, and so does dryness at the roots; that is why the worst attacks occur when the weather is cold or hot. A combination of moist air and dry roots, such as can happen in a badly managed greenhouse, may cause really crippling outbreaks of powdery mildew. Some varieties of plant are much more susceptible to mildew than others, so whenever you buy plants or seeds try to get a mildew-resistant kind.

RUST attacks a very wide range of plants, including some of the most popular inhabitants of flower borders and beds. Antirrhinums, chrysanthemums, roses, carnations, hollyhocks and many others can all be affected by rust. The symptoms of the disease are, as its name suggests, rusty spots, coloured brown, red or orange, which usually appear first on the underside of the leaves. The spots can spread quickly and disfigure the plants, which not only look unsightly but may be seriously weakened. Though the rust fungus is everywhere, different strains prefer different kinds of plant. During the past few years plant breeders have developed new varieties of some things such as antirrhinums, with inbuilt resistance to rust. It is worth paying a little extra to buy these rust-resistant varieties.

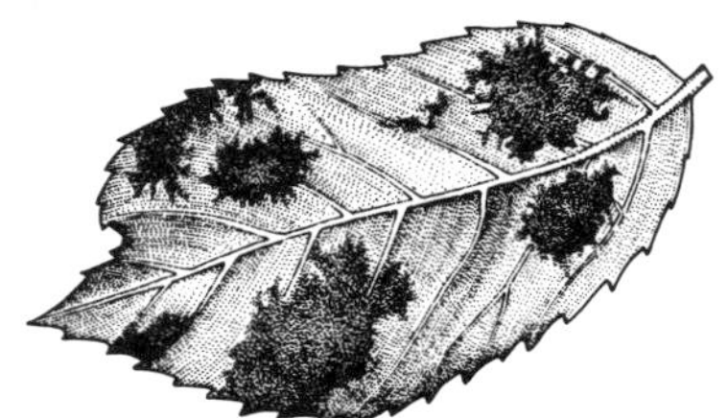

Black-spot on rose leaf

BLACK SPOT is a common disease of roses. It infects the leaves, appearing at first as pinhead-sized dark spots which soon grow into black or deep brown circles. Several spots may appear on the same leaf, sometimes overlapping each other so that there is very little green left between them. This seriously interferes with the leaf's ability to function, so that it turns yellow and falls prematurely. The infection may spread to the leaf buds and even to the shoots, causing them to die back. A bad attack may badly weaken or even kill the plant. Black spot is worst in rural areas where the air is pure. In or near industrial areas, where the atmosphere is heavily polluted, the disease is rare, because the same chemicals in the air that poison human lungs also poison the spores of black spot. Varieties of rose with thick, glossy leaves are much less likely to be attacked by this disease than those with thin, dull ones; so if you live in an area where black spot is widespread, grow only resistant varieties. It has been found that deficiency of certain minerals, particularly potash, encourages the disease, so when applying fertiliser to rose-beds always use a special rose formula, which has the correct balance of ingredients.

LEAF SPOTS of various kinds, caused by similar infections to the black-spot fungus, attack a wide range of other plants and are dealt with in the same way.

TULIP FIRE is a disease that is seen as grey patches on the leaves and causes stunting of affected plants. It can spread rapily in damp weather and will attack the flowers and the bulbs, which may develop dark patches beneath the skin and turn rotten. Badly infected plants should be removed and burnt as soon as possible. Spray the rest with a suitable fungicide to protect them.

BOTRYTIS is the name for the class of grey-moulds—tulip fire is one—which can attack almost any plant, particularly if it is soft and weak, in cold, damp conditions. It is nature's scavenger, attacking mainly dead or damaged tissue.

Virus diseases

These are of a different class from fungus diseases, and are caused by chemical-like substances which multiply in the sap-stream (often having been introduced by sucking insects, or even by an infected pruning-knife) and cause affected plants to deteriorate, usually showing striped or mottled leaves. Remove and destroy such plants; there is at present no known cure.

DISEASES AND THEIR CONTROL

Though most chmicals for the control of plant diseases are not as dangerous as those for the control of pests, *the manufacturer's instructions must be strictly obeyed in every respect*. Wash out spraying apparatus very thoroughly after use or harmful residues may be left. Also wash your hands with soap and water after mixing the chemicals or skin trouble may result. Some plants may be damaged by certain chemicals that leave others unharmed, so before using any spray make sure that it is suitable for the plant on which you intend to use it.

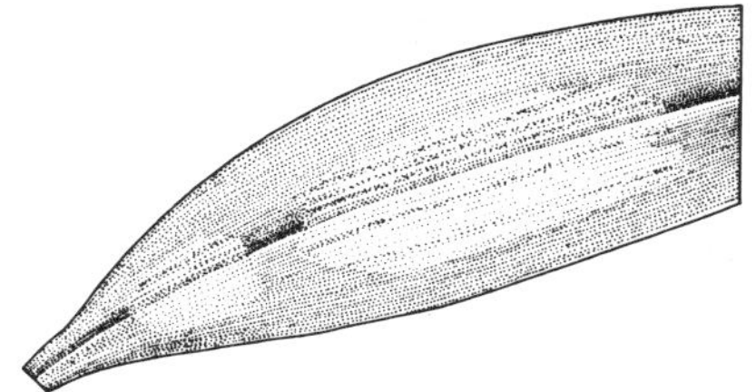

Streaked leaves from Tulip Fire

Disease	**Control**
Mildew, powdery	Spray with a systemic fungicide such as benomyl or thiophanate-methyl, dinocap (but not on dinocap-sensitive plants) or thiram, all obtainable under different brand names.
Mildew, downy	This mildew, which causes a furry instead of a powdery coating, can be controlled—if it has not gone too far—by spraying with a fungicide containing maneb or zineb.
Rust	Remove and burn affected leaves and spray the remainder with a fungicide containing maneb, zineb or thiram. More than one spraying may be necessary.
Black-spot of roses	Can be kept under control in susceptible varieties by spraying with a systemic fungicide, such as one containing benomyl or thiophanate-methyl, or with captan, maneb or zineb. Spray when first leaves unfold and repeat two or three times during summer.
Other leaf-spots	When not simply caused by sun-scorch, these are similar in symptoms and cause to black-spot and may be treated in the same way.
Tulip fire	In its early stages the disease may be controlled by spraying with a fungicide containing benomyl, thiophanate-methyl, maneb, thiram or zineb. Destroy all rotting bulbs or those showing raised black spots on them.
Botrytis	Plants badly infected with grey mould should be destroyed. Spray others with a fungicide containing benomyl, thiophanate-methyl, captan, thiram or zineb.

Flowers for Cutting

Sweet Peas

Arctotis

PERHAPS THE easiest form of gardening is to buy some flowers from a shop, take them home and arrange them in a vase or jug. Some people might object to calling that gardening, but there is no doubt that it brightens up a great many homes and brings a real sense of satisfaction to a large number of people. Many of them in these days of town-dwelling have no outside garden in any case, so they must satisfy their gardening urge by creating indoors the nearest thing they can get to a garden.

That is why there has been such an enormous increase in the number of plants in pots which people keep in their houses nowadays. Not only do the plants bring beauty of leaves and flowers into the living-room but as living things themselves they provide companionship: something to love, to look after and even to talk to. There is no greater pleasure for someone without a garden than to watch a house-plant grow and thrive, or if it falls sick to nurse it back to health again.

However, this book is not written for people without gardens, so this chapter will confine itself to flowers that are grown out in the garden and in their due season are cut and brought indoors to decorate and enrich the home. Notice the words 'in their due season'. It is no part of the purpose of this book to suggest that you try to compete with the commercial growers of cut flowers, who mass-produce a standard article, which can be bought all the year round, by the use of modern scientific techniques such as artificial day-lengthening and day-shortening. This means that plants which form their flower-buds in the spring are fooled into believing that it is spring when it is not; kinds that get the urge to flower in the summer are given a summer of artificial light; and ones that start producing flowers in the autumn are given autumn-length days by darkening the houses in which they grow, so that it is night inside while it is day outside. A vast confidence-trick is played on the plants. It is not really gardening at all but a kind of factory farming.

Part of the pleasure of raising your own cut-flowers in the garden is that there *should* be different flowers at different times, so that when you bring them indoors you bring with them something of the changing seasons. It is like having a constant change of curtains and chair-covers, but not nearly as expensive.

First let us be clear that we are not going into the rules that govern flower-arranging competitions. Many people find those rules much too rigid and some find them quite baffling, particularly when the result so often seems to be that a charming arrangement gets no prize while a monstrosity is given a gold medal. The easy way with flower-arranging is also the best way: arrange them to please yourself and forget about the rules. Better still, do not bother to learn the rules in the first place, but trust your own taste.

Some flowers that are particularly suitable for cutting do not seem to fit easily into the ordinary flower-garden. Sweet peas, for example, never look quite right in a border, but are best grown in a row with pea sticks to climb up, as a sort of temporary flowering hedge; treated in that way they make an excellent screen for a vegetable-patch, or even for a compost heap. Cut the blooms as soon as they come out; they will liven the house with their bright colours and incomparable scent.

Molucella laevis

Molucella laevis, another annual, produces spires of green bells which look as if they were made specially for flower arrangements. It does not like cold soil, so the seed should be sown rather late in the spring. There will still be time for it to make those decorative spires, which should be cut in the autumn before frosts spoil them.

Arctotis hybrids are among other flowers that seem to be specially designed for cutting and bringing indoors, where they will last in water for a long time, opening their vivid daisy-like flowers each morning and closing them at night. They too are not quite hardy and should be sown rather late, but they are so quick-growing that you will be able to cut flowers from late summer until the frosts come.

Venidium is another of the daisy family which makes a fine show as a cut flower. It will not look out of place in a bed of other annuals, but if you only want the flowers for cutting there is a lot to be said for growing it, and *Arctotis*, in rows like vegetables. In fact, many annuals for cut flower production are excellent grown in a row beside the path in the vegetable garden. They will brighten the place up, be very easy to manage, not interfere with the vegetables and at the end of the season when the ground is turned over be dug in, to do their bit towards forming humus, leaving you with pleasant memories and no regrets.

The same method can be used with Daffodils and other kinds of Narcissus for home decoration in the spring. Daffodils are so precious in the garden, as announcers that winter is over and better days are here again, that many gardeners feel it would be a crime to cut them and either go without having them indoors or buy a bunch from a shop. But if you have grown them especially in order to cut them you do not feel so much like a murderer when you do so. So when you find a clump in the garden is becoming overcrowded and have to split it up, do not throw the surplus bulbs away. Plant them, in the autumn after you have dug the ground over, beside the path in the vegetable garden or in any other odd piece of ground. It is quite a good idea to plant the bulbs rather close together; then you will get long stems, which are better for arranging in a vase. You may prefer for this purpose to plant one of the sweetly scented Narcissus varieties so that you perfume your home while you decorate it. Many of the annuals that look well in garden beds also look very well in a vase indoors; most of them bloom so freely that a few flowers cut from them will not be missed. In any case, cutting off flowers will cause others to form, and so prolong flowering; if allowed to set much seed the plants can become exhausted and die prematurely. Being annuals they are not intended to last long; and when they have produced the next generation their reason for living has gone.

African Marigold

One of the best annuals of all for decorating the home is the African Marigold, which seems to bring an extra helping of sunshine with it; its flowers are rather like round sponges and range in colour from golden, through orange, to warm, rusty brown. Before cutting any from your garden, though, see if you can detect a smell coming from them, and if so whether you like it or not. Some African Marigolds smell more than others; some people can detect no smell in them at all; some who can smell them like what they can smell and some dislike it. At any rate, whether you can smell them or not and whether you like it or not, there is a widespread belief that they give off some sort of vapour that drives away flying insects. So if you want a handsome floral decoration combined with an insect-repellant, try the African Marigold.

The Rose Mallow, or *Lavatera* as it is likely to be called on the seed-packet, is another beautiful annual specially good for cutting. It grows rapidly from seed sown in the open ground in spring, and has masses of large pink flowers which last well when cut. The flowers are produced in succession, so you can cut and come again.

There are a few easy tricks to make cut flowers last longer. First, the stem should be put into water as soon as possible after being cut. Second, the water should be continuous all the way from the vase right up through the stem, with no air-bubbles to interrupt the flow. It is surprising how quickly air can be drawn up into the cut end and spoil the continuity of the column of water. The easiest way to overcome the problem is to cut the stem a little longer than you need, and then snip off the last inch or so (2·5 cm) immediately before putting it into the water. Then there will be no time for air to get in. Secondly you can prolong the life of cut-flowers by dissolving a little sugar in the water: just enough to make it slightly sweet. To stop the sugared water going mouldy, a few drops of antiseptic may be added. You can buy packets of crystals from the flower shop, but that is all they are: sugar and antiseptic.

Thirdly, where woody-stemmed flowers like Chrysanthemums are concerned it is a good idea to beat the end of the stem with a hammer before putting it in water. This will open up more water-channels; a drop or two of antiseptic—with or without the sugar—is specially useful here, to stop the bruised stem from being infected. Fourthly, there are some species which present special problems, caused by substances in the sap which impede the taking up of water from the vase, so that even if you do all the things just suggested the flowers still wilt. The Shirley Poppy is one of those awkward kinds, so that many people never use it, lovely though it is. The trouble is that as soon as you cut the stem it exudes a milky white sap, which hardens into a rubbery lump and prevents any water from being able to get through. The remedy is quite simple. All you need to do is to put the end of the cut stems into almost boiling water for two or three minutes. This will melt the sap, and when you stand them in a vase of water, they will be able to drink it up just like other flowers. The Californian Poppy, which has the botanical name *Eschscholtzia* (and is not to be confused with the Californian Tree Poppy, which is called *Romneya*) may be treated in the same way. The flowers—which in the beautiful modern strains range in colour from gold to orange to flame colour—will last for many days, during which time they will open out in the morning and close up tight again at night, just as they do out of doors.

Lavatera

Californian Poppy

Many of the other annuals and biennials dealt with in the chapter *Seasonal furnishing* make excellent cut flowers. Some do not have long or strong enough stems, but you will not want to use them anyway. A few others will insist on shedding their petals whatever you do; but you will soon learn by trial and error which of the ones you grow have this tiresome habit and avoid using them. It is impossible to list them here, because varieties differ so widely, as do conditions in different gardens and different homes, so what is unsuitable for you may be suitable for others, and the other way round.

Absolutely reliable flowers, both for the vase and for the garden, are the many varieties of *Calendula*, the so-called English Marigold. Besides the golden-yellow ones there are orange and lemon shades, some so brilliant that they will not mix harmoniously with other flowers but demand a bowl or vase to themselves, or perhaps with a few leafy twigs to give them a little support and set them off to advantage. Another hardy annual that will never let you down, either in the garden or in the home, is that old favourite the *Cornflower*. Though there are other colours available nowadays, they cannot compare with the true old variety that gave its name to cornflower blue. Nothing looks more elegant in a vase, either by itself or with some dark foliage to contrast with the luminous blue of the flowers.

Calendula

Cornflower

That brings us to other suitable subjects for cutting, besides annual flowers, or indeed flowers at all. A piece of branch pruned from a tree or shrub and just unfolding its leaves can look extremely attractive in a long vase or large jug and will never droop but will hold itself proudly up, combining grace and strength in its design.

Then there are those shrubs, flowering on young wood, which are cut back hard each year to encourage the growth of vigorous new shoots to carry next year's flowers. Why wait till flowering is over to remove last year's branches? Why not cut some of them off as they begin to come into flower, so that you have flower-laden instead of bare shoots to decorate the home? That is an excellent way of making use of such things as Forsythia for maximum effect both inside and outside. The hardy perennials in the flower-border will provide a constant supply of cut flowers. There are very few of the tall or medium growers that cannot be used for house decoration, so long as you choose ones with strong stems and flowers that hold their heads up and look you in the face. Nothing is more depressing than flowers that hang their heads; your spirits droop with them.

There is a very good reason why you should use the border as a constant source of cut flowers. All too many people spend a great deal of time 'dead-heading'—that is cutting off dead flowers. If, instead of waiting to remove the dead from a floral graveyard, they cut off flowers while still young and attractive enough for home decoration, not only would the job be pleasanter and the home brighter but the plants would be stimulated to produce more flowers. *The younger that flowers are cut, the more new ones will appear and the longer the plant will remain in bloom.* In gathering material for winter decoration, however, it is necessary to wait for flower-heads of certain species to become mature before cutting them and letting them become dry and hard. One of the best of these is the stately *Achillea filipendula*, which has large flat heads of golden flowers held on long, stiff stems. When dry, these heads become a warm russet brown and last throughout the winter. They look very handsome in a tall vase or jug, either on their own or with other dried material to make a mixed arrangement.

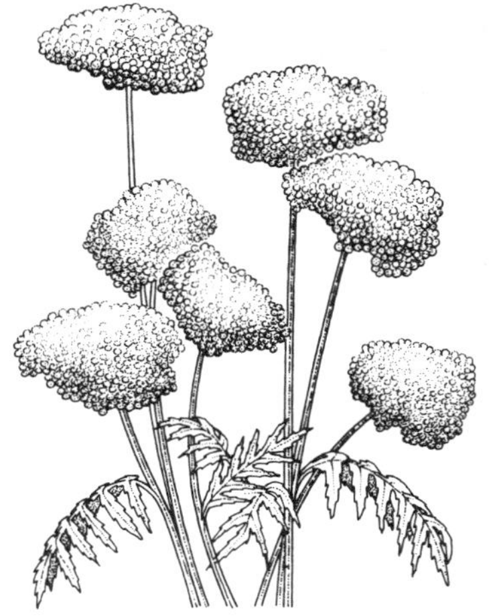

Achillea

There are many flower-heads which may be used in this way. A particularly attractive kind is known as Sea Lavender (*Limonium sinuatum*,) which grows 2 feet (60 cm) tall in the border and has large open sprays of steely blue papery flowers which last throughout the winter; there are other colours too.

Many seed-heads that can be used in this way are to be found in the border and flower-beds. Mostly they come from perennials, but some annuals yield the right sort of material too. Love-in-a-mist (*Nigella*) is grown mainly for its blue flowers, half-hidden in lace, which look very attractive in a vase of water, but if left till the bladder-like horned seed-pods appear these can be cut and will give interest to any dried arrangement.

Honesty (*Lunaria annua*) is an annual which, once established, will seed itself every year and, when its purple flowers have faded, produce flat, silvery seed-heads that last almost indefinitely and will harmonise with any other dried material, especially of a feathery nature which will contrast with its moon-like silver discs.

When gathering these heads for drying it is important to do so at the right time. They should be fully mature, but cut them before they get spoiled by autumn rain, gales or frost.

Ornamental grasses, both perennial and annual, make excellent subjects for these winter arrangements. Here timing is very important. Though the grass-flowers must be fully developed, you should not leave them a day too long or the spikes might break up and drop. Cut them as soon as they are ready and hang them up in bunches, head downwards, for a week or two to dry. A selection of suitable grasses is given in the table overleaf.

SOME DECORATIVE GRASSES

HP = Hardy perennial. HA = Hardy annual

Name	Type	Height in.	Height cm	Description
Agrostis nebulosa	HA	18	45	'Cloud Grass'. Tufted grass with dainty, many-branched flower head.
Briza maxima	HA	18	45	'Quaking-grass'. Very graceful hanging flower-spikelets.
Cortaderia selloana	HP	72	180	'Pampas Grass'. Tall, silky, silver plumes of great beauty.
Festuca glauca	HP	12	30	'Blue Fescue'. Densely tufted steel-blue foliage and flower heads.
Koeleria cristata	HP	18	45	'Crested Hair-grass'. The kind sold as 'Glauca' is very fine.
Lagurus ovatus	HA	24	60	'Hare's tail'. Soft, furry heads held on strong stems.
Milium effusum 'Aureum'	HP	36	90	'Golden Wood Millet'. Bright yellow with loose spreading flower-heads.
Molinia coerulea 'Variegata'	HP	18	45	'Striped Moor-grass'. Very handsome, with white-striped leaves.
Panicum capillare	HA	36	90	'Witch Grass'. Many-branched purple and green flower heads.
Phalaris canariensis	HA	24	60	'Canary-grass'. Dense, white-edged flower spikes on strong stalks.
Setaria italica	HA	36	90	'Fostail Millet'. Striking heads of tawny colour, very long lasting.
Stipa pennata	HP	30	75	'Feather Grass'. Thickly tufted, narrow leaves and feathery heads.
Uniola latifolia	HP	36	90	'American Wild Oats'. Handsome, tawny flower heads. Very fine.

Winter arrangement

Greenhouses etc.

THE SUBJECT of growing things under glass has been left to the end because it is doubtful whether greenhouses should be included in a book called *The Easy Garden*. If you really want your garden to be as easy as possible, you had better not have a greenhouse at all. Though it can bring a great deal of extra pleasure it brings a lot of extra work and trouble as well. It ties you down, too, because it needs constant attention, even if it is equipped with all the modern devices that are claimed by their makers to enable the greenhouse to run itself automatically. So before you buy one, ask yourself (a) whether you are willing and able to put in the extra time it demands, and (b) whether you have a friendly neighbour who can be relied upon to look after it when you go on holiday; otherwise you will either have to give up holidays or spend your time away worrying whether you will get back to find your plants dead from lack of water or cooked in their pots because someone forgot to open the ventilators on a hot day. Of course, you can tackle the problem by putting the plants outside while you are away, but if the weather turns nasty you may find that nature can behave as badly towards your plants as an unreliable neighbour. Plants leading an outdoor life can largely be left to themselves; they will usually thrive, or at least survive, and if they do not you can always blame the weather. In a greenhouse they are reliant on you, and if they fail to thrive you have nobody else to blame. In addition, pests and diseases love greenhouses, where they multiply much more rapidly than they ever could outside.

If after all that you are still interested in the subject, read on; but you have been warned.

Pot with cuttings in, covered with polythene bag

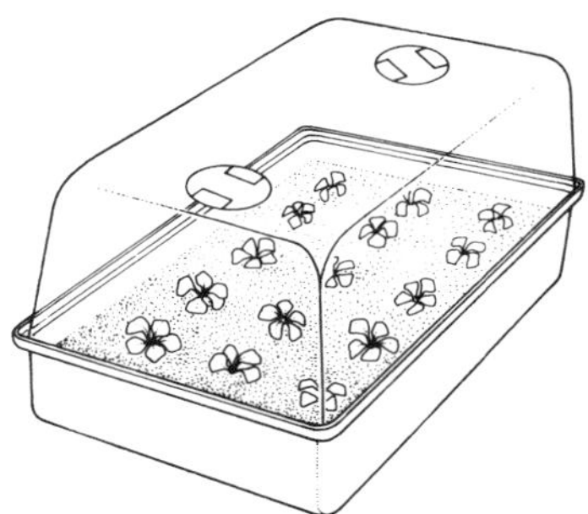

Seed tray with transparent plastic cover containing adjustable ventilators

PLASTIC COVERS

The simplest form of protection is a plastic bag placed over a pot containing cuttings or seedlings to prevent them from drying out. Then there are the domed plastic lids designed to be fixed over seed-trays. These also prevent cuttings or seedlings from drying out. Choose ones with adjustable ventilators, so that humidity can be controlled. The value of such covers is not to control temperature but to keep the moisture content of the air under them constant and prevent the compost from drying out, so that it needs frequent watering and may become soggy.

CLOCHES

To protect against heat loss during cold nights, cloches are a great help, making it possible to bring somewhat tender plants through the winter successfully. Their greatest value is in the vegetable garden, where their use in the spring enables such things as lettuces, radishes, stump-rooted carrots and even early peas to be sown and gathered weeks before it would be possible to do so in the open ground.

Some small-growing crops can spend their life under cloches till it is time for them to be used, but in most cases the cloches are removed when the weather is past its worst, and the plants mature in the open. An exception is in the case of strawberries (best grown as a vegetable-garden crop, as described on page 104), which do better if they are allowed to form their flower-buds in the open and then covered with large-sized cloches to protect the blossoms from late frosts. Cloches are on sale in a variety of shapes and sizes, but there are basically two types: glass and plastic. As usual in this imperfect world, one is not superior to the other on all points; there are things to be said for and against each of them.

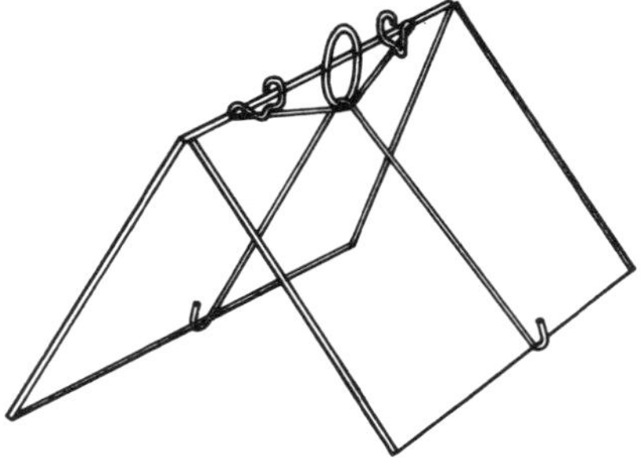

Glass cloche

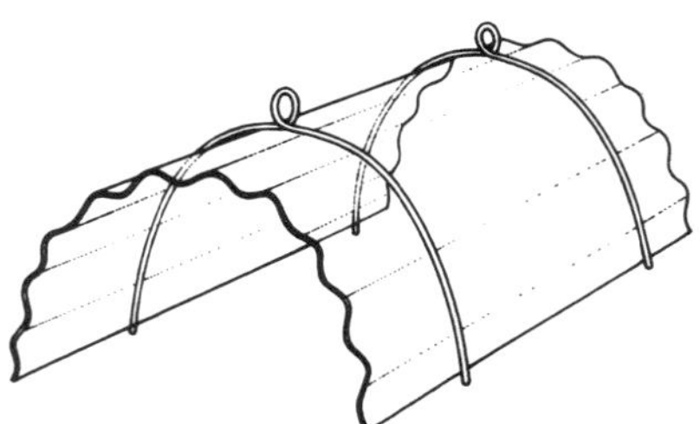

Plastic cloche

Glass cloches are usually shaped like an inverted V, made up of two rectangular pieces of glass held together either by wire or by a metal clip at the top. They are placed end to end in a row with as little space as possible between them—so as not to let in the cold, or let out the heat—and closed at each end of the row with a vertical pane of glass held in place by a stake driven firmly into the ground.

The advantages of glass cloches are that they (a) keep the heat in well, (b) are stable and not easily blown over, and (c) do not deteriorate. Their disadvantages are that they are (a) heavy to move and (b) easily broken.

Plastic cloches are usually rounded, and pegged into the ground with wire hoops. Some are reinforced with wire-netting. Their advantages are that they are (a) generally cheaper, and (b) lighter to carry. Their disadvantages are (a) that they can be blown away in a high wind, and (b) that plastic tends to deteriorate through exposure to sunlight; the ultraviolet rays turn it brittle and it breaks very easily.

FRAMES

A rather more ambitious form of protection than cloches is the garden frame, which is particularly useful in the early spring for giving a little bit of additional comfort to plants which, though they do not need extra heat, will grow quicker and better if they are protected from frost. It can also provide a safe place for some plants that might be killed by cold and wet outside.

Most frames have a glass top, and sides made of some thicker material which is a poor thermal conductor and so keeps in the heat. The simplest structure is an old wooden box with the bottom knocked out and a sheet of glass placed over the top; a small flat piece of wood screwed to the outside at the centre of each side, so that it projects upwards slightly, will keep the glass in place but enable it to be lifted out easily when the plants need attention.

If the sides can be sawn so that the back is higher than the front, the rain will run off instead of going into the frame. Earth banked up against the outside of the frame will help to reduce heat loss still further.

The most solid and long-lasting garden-frame was the old-fashioned kind with brick walls laid in cement mortar on concrete foundations. On that was fitted a glazed wooden light with the glass set in putty. In some types the light was made to slide in grooves to allow ventilation; in others the light was hinged at the top and could be propped open with wooden wedges, cut in steps to allow different amounts of opening according to the temperature and wind. Such structures are rarely built nowadays, because of the labour and expense involved. However, there are modern materials which can be used instead of brickwork for the walls of the frame and are much cheaper and easier to build: breeze blocks, concrete slabs, and even reinforced plastic, which is the best material yet for preventing heat-loss. You can buy a whole package, easy and quick to assemble, including walls, bolts to fix them together, and a glazed top-light either of timber (Western red cedar is best) or of metal (either galvanised steel or aluminium alloy). There are also some excellent new glass-to-ground frames which give maximum light all round, and so produce stocky plants instead of tall, drawn ones. They are also portable, so they can be stored away when not in use.

In the past few years, electrical soil-warming cables have been produced which enable a certain amount of artificial heat to be used

Garden frame

Cineraria 'Spring Beauty'

in even the smallest and simplest frame, and so greatly extend the number of plants that can be grown. However, with heating bills—especially when electricity is used as the source of warmth—going up all the time, we shall not deal with any form of artificially heated frame. That would not only be beyond the scope of this book but contradict its title. The easy garden must not only be easy to manage and easy on the muscles, but easy on the pocket too. If you are thinking of going beyond a cold frame and having a full-sized greenhouse, first ask yourself (a) why you want it, and (b) how much you will use it. Is it because friends or neighbours have one? That is not a good enough reason. You will be taking on another family to look after (a collection of plants in a greenhouse is a family of dependents) and losing some of your freedom. That envied friend or neighbour may secretly be envying you for not having the same ties and responsibilities and being able to go away when you want.

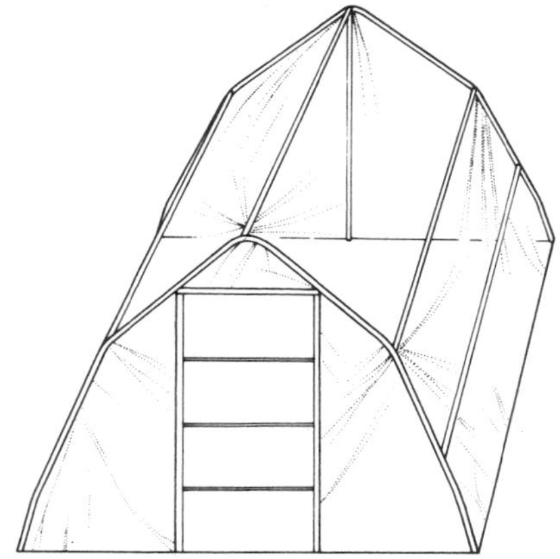

Plastic covered dutch-light greenhouse

The second question is a clinching one. Thousands of greenhouses are only used for a small part of the year, maybe to raise a few bedding plants; for months on end they house nothing but one or two scruffy plants on their last legs, a collection of old junk and an assortment of earwigs and other creepy-crawlies. They are a waste of space and money most of the year.

Perhaps the best reason for having a greenhouse is to be able to gather your own fresh salad vegetables when it is not possible to grow them in the open garden and the ones in the shops are expensive. The two most rewarding kinds to grow are probably tomatoes, in the summer and autumn, and lettuces in the winter and spring.

If you intend to grow them not for the simple satisfaction of eating your own produce and enjoying its superior flavour but because you want to feel you are saving money, you must buy something cheap; otherwise it will never pay for itself.

Primula obconica

DUTCH-LIGHT

This is the cheapest practical type, covered with plastic down to ground level to give maximum light to the plants.

As we have seen earlier, transparent plastic does not last, however careful you are to avoid tearing it. The ultra-violet rays in sunlight break down its structure and it becomes brittle and goes into holes. Some plastics are treated so as to reduce the damaging effect of the rays, and they do last a little longer; but it is doubtful whether the extra cost of the treated material is justified by its slightly longer life. All plastic has to be replaced sooner or later.

For the easy garden, where, as we have seen, unnecessary work is eliminated by the principle of *making the first cost—of money, time and effort—the last*, the only really satisfactory material for greenhouses at present is glass. Maybe some day someone will invent a totally new plastic that lasts for ever, but that day seems a long way off. Apart from the 'Dutch light' pattern just dealt with (page 143), which can also be bought in a glass version, there are basically three types of greenhouse (apart from the round, modern ones, which are still in the expensive and gimmicky stage and are hardly suitable for such a practical down-to-earth book as *The Easy Garden*).

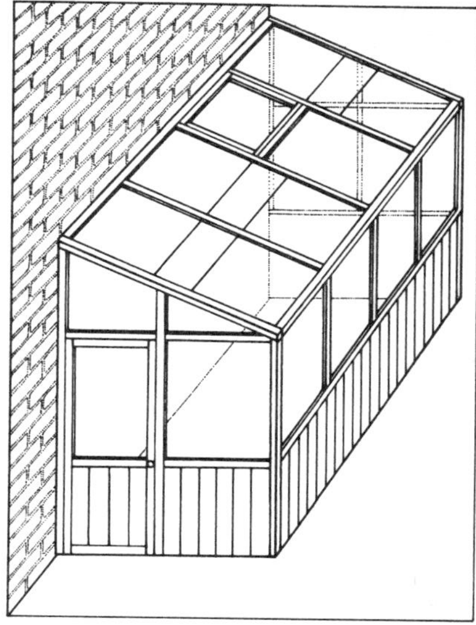

Wooden lean-to greenhouse

LEAN-TO

This is the kind built against a wall. Not only does this save on materials (only one roof-slope has to be built instead of two) and make a very strong and rigid structure, but the lean-to has certain advantages for some situations and some plants. And, of course, it has certain disadvantages too. *Advantages* are (a) that it retains heat very well; the sun's rays strike through the glass on to the wall, which absorbs the warmth and gives it out gradually again during the night—a very practical use of solar energy; and (b) that it is the perfect design for a plant room attached to the house; if the position is right, a window between living-room or kitchen and lean-to enables the plants to be watched from inside the house as they grow. *Disadvantages* are (a) that a lean-to must only be built against a south-facing wall or the plants will be starved of sun; and (b) that with the light coming from one direction some plants can become drawn and leggy.

There is a sort of variation of the lean-to known as the three-quarter span greenhouse in which the roof-slope does not go right back to the wall but to a ridge-board a short distance in front of it; from that ridge a second, much shorter portion of roof slopes down to the wall. This gives a certain amount of extra light from the wall side, but the increased cost of the extra roof-slope makes the three-quarter span hardly worthwhile.

SPAN-ROOF

These greenhouses are much the commonest type, and best for general purposes. They are obtainable in a wide variety of sizes and are sent in sections, together with diagrams and sets of instructions which make the job of erecting the house and glazing it quite easy. (A worthwhile tip: when lifting glass, wear stout gloves or wrap thick cloth or several layers of newspaper round the edge; that will prevent painful cuts from razor-sharp glass). *Advantages* of the span-roof house are (a) that it can be put in any suitable part of the garden; and (b) that with light coming through the glass on all sides, growth tends to be even, so that the plants are sturdy and upright. *Disadvantages are* (a) that, with a larger relative area of glass, heat-loss can be worse on a cold night; and (b) that for the same reason the house can become oven-hot very quickly on a sunny day. Most greenhouses have glass down to about waist level, i.e. the level of the staging on which the plants stand. Below that are walls, which may be of brick, concrete slabs or wood panels supplied with the greenhouse. The majority of greenhouses are of wood. Western red cedar is best because it is rot-proof.

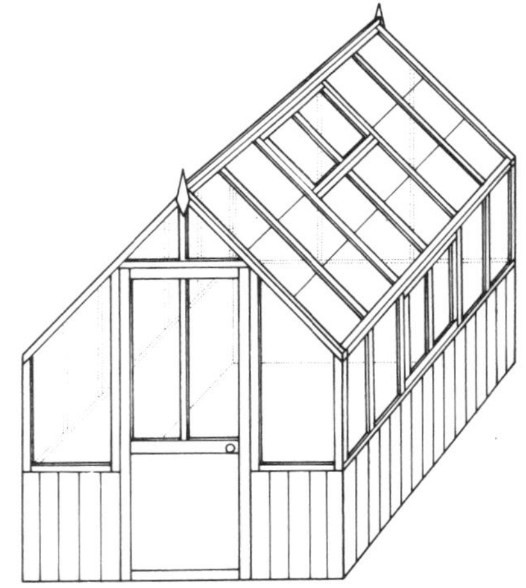

Wooden span-roof greenhouse

METAL FRAMED

The most trouble-free greenhouses of all are the modern ones made of light metal, with the glass set in a waterproof compound and clipped into place. Those made of galvanised steel are slightly cheaper, but those made of aluminium are best; once they have been erected they need no maintenance at all. The one pictured is the easy gardener's ideal. It has glass down to the ground, so that tomatoes or chrysanthemums can be planted, but staging, obtainable as an optional extra, can be added to hold plants in pots.

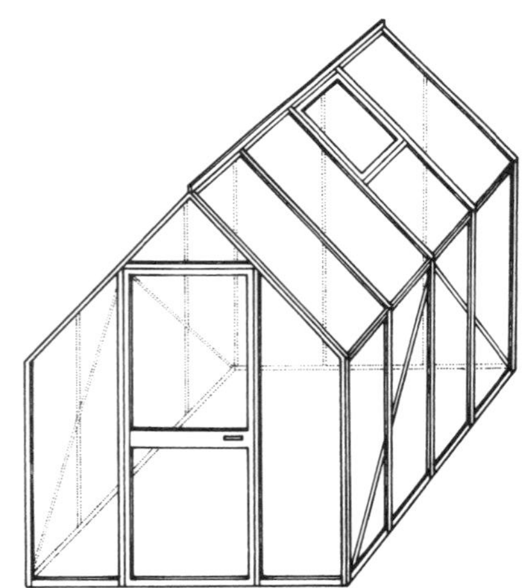

Light aluminium greenhouse

SITING

When deciding where to place a greenhouse in the garden, the most important thing is that it should be right out in the open, never under the shade of a tree. The parts of the world that are cold enough for a greenhouse to be worth having all lie in latitudes where winter days are short. The sort of plants which benefit from greenhouse protection, on the other hand, all come from places that are warmer, which means nearer to the equator, which in turn means that they never have such short days. Therefore you must do everything you can to make sure that the greenhouse gets every bit of light that is available during those short daylight hours of winter. If you cannot avoid the shade of a tree entirely, make it a deciduous rather than an evergreen one, because deciduous trees at least lose their leaves in the winter and therefore do not cast such a dark shadow. The long sides of a greenhouse should run east and west, to catch the most light during the winter; and in the summer only the side facing south will need to be shaded.

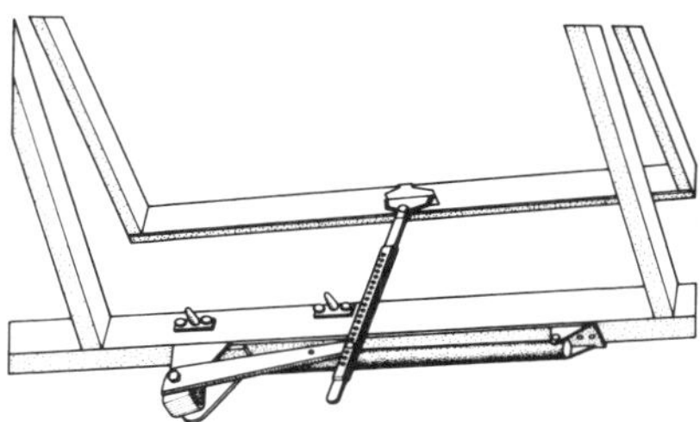

Automatic vent opener

VENTILATION

The chief killer of greenhouse plants in winter is wet roots during a cold spell. In summer the chief killer is dryness coupled with heat. The air inside an average small greenhouse can heat up with alarming speed on a sunny day and cook the plants. Ventilators must be opened before that happens, so that the hot air can escape. That used to mean keeping a constant watch on the temperature; or worse still having to open the ventilators before you went off to work, which was too early, and closing them when you got back, which was too late. Now the problem is overcome by fixing an automatic opener, which contains a substance that expands with heat and opens the ventilator. It needs no electricity but is powered simply by temperature rise and fall.

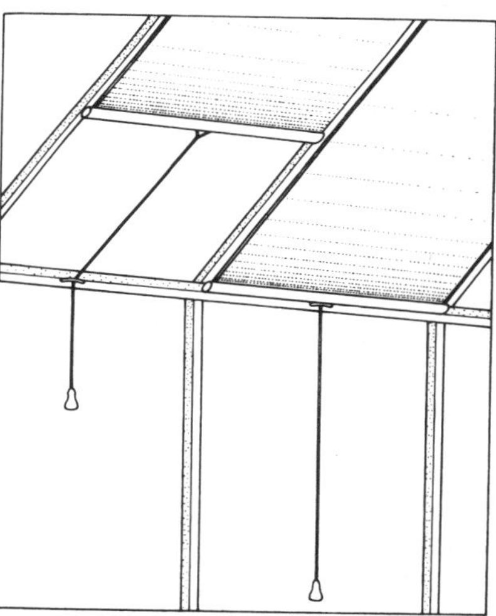

Interior roller blinds

SHADING

The roof-glass can be shaded during the summer by brushing or spraying on a compound that only needs mixing with water—or blinds can be fitted, either internally or externally. The exterior type is more efficient, but more expensive.

MOISTURE CONTROL

One of the greatest problems during sunny summer days is how to keep sufficient moisture in the air. As we have seen, the temperature in the greenhouse must not be allowed to rise too high before the ventilators are opened; but unfortunately as the hot air escapes it takes the moisture with it. The result can be disastrous for the plants, most of which hate a dry atmosphere (which, to make matters worse, is loved by some of the worst greenhouse pests such as red spider). Two things can be done to reduce the danger. First, the ventilators should be opened a little way *before* the air in the greenhouse has become too hot, and the opening increased as the outside temperature rises. *Remember that the hotter the air has been allowed to get, the more moisture it will take with it when it is finally released.* After the hottest part of the day is over, start closing down the ventilators gradually so that they are shut before the evening. It is here that the automatic opener is such a blessing, because it varies the opening according to the heat. Secondly, the greenhouse should be damped down in hot weather, which simply means watering paths and spraying walls, staging and leaves in the morning. There are automatic devices, electrically operated, which spray a fine mist into the air when the humidity drops below a certain point, but they are rather expensive. Besides, when dryness becomes a problem, there are likely to be restrictions on using water.

Water

Within the next few years, as demand increases, water will become more and more precious. It is likely that in many places the use of mains water for private gardening will be forbidden by law for longer and longer periods during the driest part of the year, just when it is most needed. So it is a sensible precaution to make yourself a bit less dependent on water from the tap. Save as much rain water as possible, by collecting it in the greenhouse gutters and leading it through downpipes into rainwater butts. The best are those made of plastic, which do not heat up as the old galvanised ones used to do, causing the water to evaporate. Rainwater is much better for plants than tap-water, which can be very hard. Conditions vary so much that there is no simple answer to the question how often to water. The only unbreakable rule is this: *never water a wet plant.*

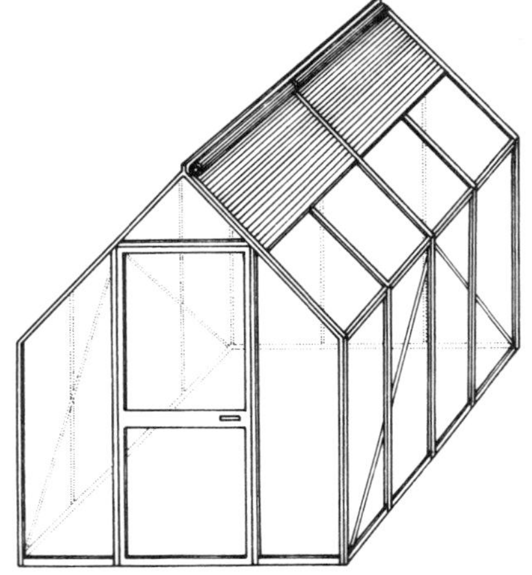

Exterior roller blinds

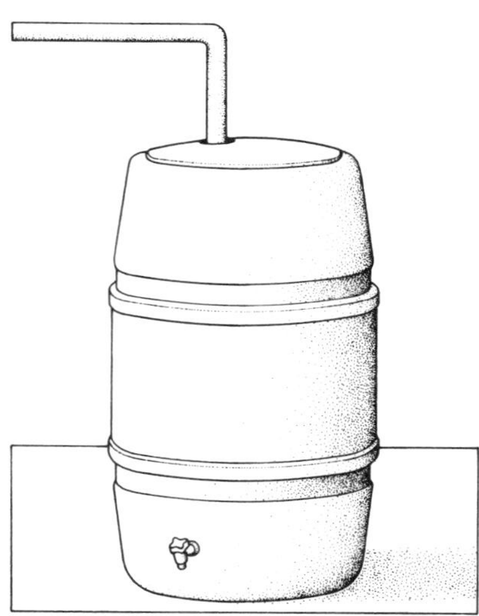

Plastic rainwater butt

HEATING

Since hot houses—or even warm houses—are beyond the scope of this book, we shall deal only with those which use little or no artificial heat. There are two types: the *Cold House*, which is left unheated throughout the year, and the *Cool House*, which is heated only in the winter, to stop the temperature falling below about 7°C (45°F). To keep temperatures above that becomes extremely expensive and requires artificial heat all or most of the year. Every 3°C extra doubles the cost; so that to maintain 10°C would cost twice as much, and 13°C four times as much, as the modest 7°C of a cool house.

Cold House

Since this is never given any artificial heat, the temperature inside it will drop to freezing point, or even below, in really icy weather. In spite of this, plants will not suffer so badly as they would outside. There are two reasons: (a) some of the heat they give off is reflected back from the glass instead of vanishing into the sky, and (b) they can be kept drier, so that they are not in such danger from icing-up.

The proper use of a cold house is to extend the season of things that are quite hardy in the open but are several weeks earlier in the spring, and later in the autumn, if grown under glass. Spring bulbs can be coaxed into flower while it is still winter outside, and autumn chrysanthemums will go on blooming after those in the open have been finished off by frost. Lettuces sown inside in the autumn will be ready to cut a month or more before those sown in the spring; tomatoes planted several weeks ahead of those in the open will give earlier fruit; and later too, because they will go on producing when frost has put paid to outdoor ones. Strawberries in pots can be brought indoors and will fruit weeks before those outside. Carrots may be sown in late winter to give an early crop.

Cool House

To maintain a minimum temperature of 7°C during the winter there are many types of heater to choose from. The cheapest are those which use paraffin, and the most expensive (but most labour-saving) are thermostatically-controlled electric ones.

In addition to all the things that can be grown in cold houses, there are many other plants that a cool house makes possible. A brief selection is given on p. 148.

Fuchsia

Cyclamen

SOME EASY PLANTS FOR THE COOL HOUSE

A = Annual. B = Biennial. Bu = Bulb. C = Corn. Cl. = Climber.
E = Evergreen. P = Perennial. S = Shrub. T = Tuber.

Name	Type	Height in.	Height cm	Flowering time	Flowering colour	Description
Abutilon hybrids	S	30	75	Su	Various	Veined bell flowers.
Ardisia crispa	ES	36	90	Su	White	Bright red winter berries.
Asclepias curassavica	EP	30	75	Su	Orange	Dense heads of bright flowers.
Azalea, Indian	ES	18	45	Sp	Various	Gorgeous, long-lasting display.
Begonia fuchsioides	ES	48	120	A-Sp	Pink	Many other kinds available.
Billbergia nutans	P	18	45	Sp	Mixed	Hanging blue and pink flowers.
Calceolaria hybrids	B	12	30	Sp	Mixed	Pouched red spotted yellow flowers.
Capsicum annum	A	12	30	Su	White	'Pepper'. Orange or red fruits.
Cineraria varieties	B	30	75	W-Sp	Various	Masses of brightly coloured daisies.
Clianthus puniceus	S	36	90	Su	Scarlet	'Lobster Claw'. Vivid and striking.
Clivia miniata	P	18	45	Sp-Su	Orange	Trumpet-flowers in large heads.
Crinum × powellii	Bu	18	45	Su-A	Pink	Shiny leaves and trumpet flowers.
Cyclamen persicum	C	8	20	W-Sp	Various	Large flowered varieties in many colours.
Diplacus glutinosus	ES	24	60	Sp-A	Orange	Trumpet flowers: also crimson etc.
Eucomis bicolor	Bu	18	45	Su	Green	Unusual purple-edged flowers.
Francoa ramosa	P	30	75	Su	White	Sprays of flowers; also pink.
Freesia hybrids	C	24	60	W-Sp	Various	Scented flowers in many colours.
Fuchsia hybrids	S	48	120	Su-A	Various	Popular flowers in great variety.
Gomphrena globosa	A	12	30	Sp-Su	Pink etc.	'Globe amaranth'. Round heads.
Haemanthus multiflorus	Bu	24	60	Sp	Red	'Blood Lily'. Spheres of flowers.

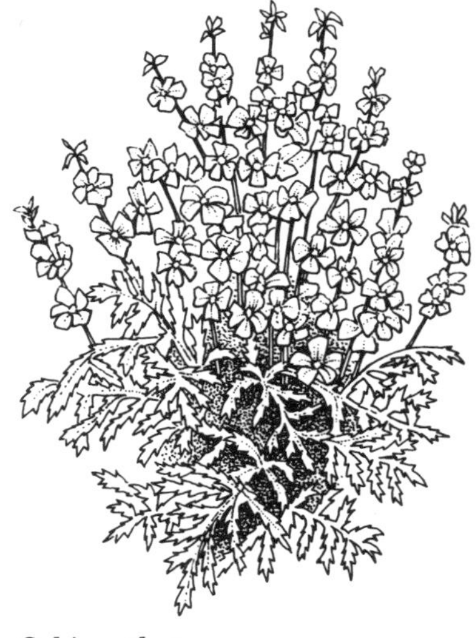

Schizanthus

Name	Type	Height in.	Height cm	Flowering time	Flowering colour	Description
Heliotropium hybrids	S	24	60	Su-A	Lavender	'Cherry pie'. Scented flowers.
Hippeastrum hybrids	Bu	18	45	W-Su	Various	Big trumpets in warm colours.
Hoya carnosa	Cl	60	150	Su-A	White	Scented, waxy star flowers.
Impatiens hybrids	P	8	20	Sp-W	Various	'Busy Lizzie'. Vivid flowers.
Ipomoea varieties	Cl	84	210	Su-A	Blue	'Morning Glory'. Serene colour.
Lachenalia aloides	Bu	12	30	Sp	Yellows	'Cape Cowslip'. Red markings.
Lantana camara	S	36	90	Su-A	Gold etc.	Bright reds and pinks too.
Lapageria rosea	E Cl	96	240	Su-A	Rose	'Chilean Bell-flower'. Large bells.
Lilium species	Bu	60	150	Sp-A	Various	Hundreds of lovely varieties.
Nerine sarniensis	Bu	24	60	A	Red	'Guernsey Lily'. Glowing colour.
Pelargonium hybrids	P	24	60	Sp-W	Various	'Geranium'. Very many kinds.
Polianthes tuberosa	T	36	90	Sp-A	White	'Tuberose'. Highly scented flowers.
Primula obconica	P	12	30	W-Su	Various	Best greenhouse species.
Schizanthus varieties	A	36	90	Su-A	Various	'Butterfly Flower'. Spectacular.
Sinningia speciosa	T	10	25	Su-A	Various	'Gloxinia'. Large velvet flowers.
Solanum capsicastrum	ES	18	45	Su	White	'Winter Cherry'. Red berries.
Sprekelia formosissima	Bu	18	45	Sp	Crimson	Lovely orchid-like flowers.
Streptocarpus hybrids	P	12	30	Sp-A	Various	'Cape Primrose'. Many colours.
Vallota speciosa	Bu	18	45	Su	Scarlet	'Scarborough Lily'. Dazzling.
Veltheimia capensis	Bu	12	30	Sp	Pink	Long spike of speckled flowers.
Zantedeschia aethiopica	P	30	75	Sp-Su	White	'Arum Lily'. Great for cutting.

Pelargonium

Index of Botanical Names

General Index